GOLDEN TALES OF GREECE

Golden Tales

The Stories of Perseus, Jasor

Retold by Compton Mackenzie

# of Greece
Achilles and Theseus

Illustrated by William Stobbs

ALDUS BOOKS · JUPITER BOOKS

SBN 490 00321 4

First published in this edition in 1974 by
Aldus Books Limited, Aldus House,
17 Conway Street, London W1P 6BS
and Jupiter Books, 167 Hermitage Road,
London N4 1LZ

Printed and bound in Yugoslavia by
Mladinska Knjiga, Ljubljana

The Story of
PERSEUS

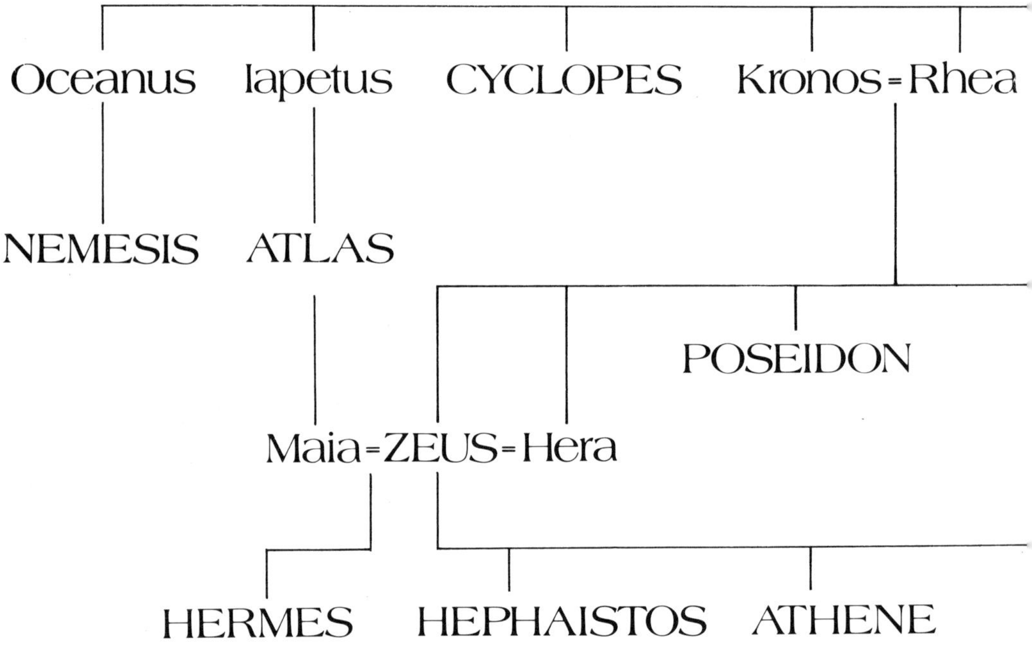

Oceanus
Iapetus
CYCLOPES
Kronos = Rhea
NEMESIS
ATLAS
POSEIDON
Maia = ZEUS = Hera
HERMES
HEPHAISTOS
ATHENE

GODS AND GODDESSES

IN THE STORY OF PERSEUS

Uranus = Gaea = Pontus

Phorcys = Ceto

Nereus = Doris

THE NEREIDS

THE GORGONS

THE GRAIAE

HADES

= DANAE

= Alcmene

PERSEUS

HERAKLES

This family tree shows the gods and goddesses of ancient Greece, and the demi-gods and mortals related to them, whose lives are linked with that of Perseus, the hero of this story of once upon a time. Those whose names are in capitals—for example, ATHENE and HERAKLES—played a direct part in Perseus' adventures. Those whose names are not in capitals—such as Alcmene, mother of HERAKLES—take their places in the tree as links in the line of descent from Gaea, the Earth-mother. It was believed in that world of long ago that Gaea was created out of Chaos. She brought forth Uranus (Heaven) and Pontus (Sea), by both of whom she then had children. From her were descended all the other gods and goddesses of Greece.

The fisherman brought the chest ashore

Perseus

Just over fifty years ago, I was standing with some companions on a small deserted island off the coast of Asia Minor. We were waiting anxiously for a signal from a Greek messenger hidden in a grove of olives on the shore of the mainland. He was to send us news of what was happening in Turkey, which was then at war with Britain. But the signal did not come. We were on the point of boarding our launch to return to the island of Lesbos when we saw a wooden chest floating toward us. We waded into the sea and dragged the chest ashore. Inside it, we found a young woman holding a tiny baby.

She was a beautiful Greek girl whose husband had been killed by the Turks. Terrified that her child too would be killed and that she herself would be carried away to a Turkish harem, she had managed to hide until she saw an empty chest bobbing about beside the shore. She had climbed into the chest with her baby and had been carried across the narrow stretch of water to the island, where we were able to rescue her.

Some five thousand years earlier, a fisherman on the shore of the island of Seriphos, in that beautiful archipelago called the Cyclades, had, like us, seen a chest floating past. He had netted it and brought it ashore.

He had forced open the lid and found a radiantly beautiful young woman with a baby in her arms. The story I am going to tell you now is the story of that earlier woman and her baby.

Once upon a time, a mighty warrior whose name was Abas ruled over the kingdom of Argolis. King Abas had twin sons called Proitos and Akrisios, who had hated each other ever since they were children. So when King Abas realized that his death was approaching he tried to think of a way to bequeath his kingdom that would avoid a civil war between his twin heirs. At last he decided that Proitos and Akrisios should rule Argolis in alternate years.

King Abas was too optimistic in thinking that his solution would prevent civil war. After his death, each of the twin monarchs of Argolis began plotting to secure the throne for himself. Proitos was not yet married, but Akrisios had a wife, and a beautiful young daughter called Danaë. When it was his turn to reign in Argolis, Akrisios accused his brother of having tried to carry off Danaë and marry her. He succeeded in stirring up the Argives (the people of Argos, capital of the kingdom) against Proitos. Proitos, fearing for his safety, fled to the court of Iobates, the King of Lycia. There he fell in love with Anteia, the King's daughter, and, in the course of time, married her.

After the marriage, King Iobates decided to invade Argolis with a Lycian army to put his new son-in-law back on the throne. There was a fierce battle between the Lycians and the Argives, but, after much slaughter on both sides, the opposing armies grew tired of fighting and decided to call it a draw, leaving the twin Kings of Argolis to come to terms with one another. It was clear to Proitos and Akrisios that ruling Argolis in alternate years would never work, and finally they agreed to partition the kingdom. Akrisios was to have Argos and Proitos was to have the town of Tiryns. Proitos secured the services of seven Cyclopes, and these one-eyed giants encircled Tiryns with massive stone walls, large parts of which still survive today.

Although Akrisios now reigned secure on the throne of Argos, he was distressed that he had no son to inherit his realm. So he consulted an oracle to find out if he would ever have an heir. The oracle was extremely discouraging. Akrisios would never have a son. But, worse still, he would have a grandson and at the hands of his grandson he would meet his death.

Akrisios decided that the sooner he made it impossible for his daughter Danaë to have a child the safer he would feel. He threatened suitors for her hand with death, and they all escaped from Argos and its neighborhood as quickly as possible.

Then Akrisios built a tower with a bronze door, and set savage hounds to guard it. In this tower he immured his beautiful young daughter, to spend the rest of her life without so much as seeing a man.

Akrisios consulted an oracle

But Danaë was saved by her beauty from lifelong imprisonment in the tower. Zeus, the father of gods and men, beheld and loved her. Savage hounds were powerless against Zeus; bronze doors were useless. One night, Danaë was tossing restlessly on her couch, not knowing whether she was awake or half asleep and dreaming, when suddenly her room was filled with golden light, and from the roof she saw a shower of gold descending. She was not dreaming. In that shower of gold Zeus himself came to her.

Nine months later, Danaë gave birth to a baby who was to become as famous as any of the Heroes of Hellas of once upon a time. His name was Perseus.

Akrisios was almost mad with anger when Perseus was born. He refused to believe that Zeus was the baby's father. He even imagined that his hated twin brother Proitos had somehow contrived to get into the tower and seduce Danaë. Only fear of the penalty the inexorable goddess Nemesis might exact for the crime stopped him from killing his own daughter. He thought and thought of how to put Danaë and the baby Perseus to death without the guilt of bloodshed upon his hands.

At last he hit upon a plan. He put Danaë and Perseus into a chest and nailed down the heavy lid. That night, he ordered two of his slaves to carry the chest down to the shore and set it adrift.

Akrisios had persuaded himself that if his daughter and her baby son were drowned their deaths would not be his responsibility. When the chest sank, it would just be a shipwreck like many another.

But Zeus had no intention of letting his son be drowned. He was resolved that Perseus should one day be one of the great Heroes of Hellas. So he asked his brother Poseidon, who ruled the sea as he himself ruled heaven and earth, to order the sea-nymphs to guide the floating chest to the island of Seriphos. There Diktys the fisherman saw the chest floating past, netted it, and brought it ashore.

Diktys was no ordinary fisherman. He was the younger brother of Polydektes, the King of Seriphos. He was unmarried, and much more interested in fishing than in court ceremonies. He lived in a lonely house at the other end of the island from his brother's palace. To this house he took Danaë and the baby Perseus, and for a week or two he said nothing to the King about their arrival on Seriphos. Then he became worried in case somebody found out that he was sheltering them, and thought it prudent to tell King Polydektes about the chest and its surprising contents.

Polydektes, too, was unmarried and he was much attracted by Danaë's beauty. He suggested that she and her infant son should come to live in his palace. Danaë begged to be allowed to remain with Diktys. She saw the way Polydektes looked at her and was afraid he would try to make love to her once she was in his palace. She would have liked to explain to him that Zeus was the

Two slaves set the chest adrift

father of her son, but she knew he would not believe her story of the shower of gold. Even her father had not believed it. However, Polydektes reluctantly agreed that she should remain in his brother's house.

That evening Danaë told Diktys how she had been visited by Zeus, the father of gods and men, and had borne his son. Diktys was sure that Danaë was telling him the truth. He felt a great responsibility for her and for her half-divine infant son. He made up his mind to bring up Perseus to be a great Hellenic Hero.

From time to time during the boyhood of Perseus, King Polydektes tried to persuade Danaë to marry him. Perseus, who had no desire to live in the palace, was glad that his mother always refused the King's proposals.

Like all the Hellenic Heroes, Perseus was a great athlete. He threw the javelin and the discus unerringly; he could outbox anybody in Seriphos, run faster, and jump higher. By the time he was sixteen years old he was the champion athlete of Seriphos.

By this time Danaë was a little over thirty and still as beautiful as she had been when Zeus had come to her in the tower. King Polydektes still wanted to marry her, but Danaë still refused him. Polydektes felt that he had no chance of winning Danaë's hand so long as Perseus remained in Seriphos to influence his mother. He wondered how to get Perseus away from Seriphos and at last he thought of a plan. He announced to his subjects that he intended to propose marriage to one of the daughters of King Pelops. That would involve going to the Peloponnese, the Island of King Pelops, the greatest breeder of horses in all Hellas. He could not go to the court of Pelops without taking a gift of horses. So he asked those of his subjects who could afford it to contribute to the gift.

Polydektes had no intention of going to the Peloponnese to ask for the hand of one of King Pelops' daughters. What he intended was to find a way of making Perseus leave Seriphos so that he could continue to press Danaë to marry him. So he waited until many of the people of Seriphos had offered to contribute horses, and then sent for Perseus and asked him what he intended to give.

Perseus was angered by what he felt was the King's deliberate desire to mortify him in front of the court. He was at that difficult age when youth is becoming manhood, and when the self-consciousness of youth tries to behave with the self-assurance of manhood. It was all too easy for Polydektes to embarrass him.

"I can't afford to give you a horse," Perseus told Polydektes, "you might as well ask me to give you the head of the Gorgon Medusa."

(This was simply a way of saying that it was impossible for him to provide a horse for Polydektes.)

"The Gorgon's head?" Polydektes repeated. "That would be a fine offering, but I fear that is much too difficult and dangerous an exploit for a youth . . . a young man of your age," he added with a crafty smile.

Horses for King Polydektes

And, of course, this had just the effect he wanted on the proud young Perseus.

"You think I am too young to go in search of the Gorgon's head?" Perseus demanded. "I will prove to you how wrong you are."

With what seemed like youthful boasting, Perseus strode out of the King's palace, flushing with anger as he heard the laughter of Polydektes' obsequious courtiers ringing out behind him.

Polydektes chuckled to himself. He did not imagine for a moment that young Perseus would get anywhere near the Gorgons, much less be able to cut off Medusa's head. But the search would keep Perseus away from Seriphos for a long time, perhaps for ever.

Perseus set off toward his home. He felt sure that when Diktys and his mother heard what he had undertaken they would both do their utmost to dissuade him from setting out on so dangerous a quest. As he walked along, he tried to remember all he had been told about the three sisters called the Gorgons. Two of them—Sthenno and Euryale—were immortal, but the youngest—Medusa—was mortal. She had once been beautiful, but she had offended against the goddess Athene who, to punish her, had changed her beauty into an appalling hideousness. She now had snakes instead of hair. Her teeth were very large and her tongue stuck out of her mouth as if to lap human blood. The mere sight of that horrible face turned people to stone.

As he realized what an impossible task he had undertaken Perseus was shocked at his own folly. But he was much too proud to consider backing out, and he knelt to invoke the aid of the almighty Zeus, the lord of heaven and earth, his father.

When he rose to his feet he saw beside him a woman with a helmet, and carrying a shield and a spear. Perseus knew at once that this was the goddess Athene, who was believed to have sprung fully armed from the head of Zeus. He went down upon his knees again, kneeling in reverence before her.

The goddess bade him rise and looked kindly at him with her great, gray eyes.

"You wish to bring home the head of the Gorgon Medusa. I wish to have that head for myself and I will help you to carry out the hard task you have set yourself. Go as quickly as you can to the island of Samos. Call to me when you reach Samos and I will appear to you again and give you my commands."

As she spoke the goddess vanished.

When Perseus reached home and told his mother and Diktys about his encounter with Athene they did not, after all, oppose his heroic enterprise. They both felt sure that the protection of Zeus, which had brought Danaë and her baby son safely to Seriphos, would guard that baby son now that he was a youth. Diktys promised he would do all he could to prevent his brother Polydektes from annoying Danaë too much in Perseus' absence.

The goddess Athene appeared to Perseus

Two or three days later a merchant ship, bound for the islands off the coast of what today we call Asia Minor, put in at Seriphos, and Perseus was able to work his passage to Samos by becoming one of its oarsmen. When the ship reached port in Samos, he disembarked and made his way to the temple of Athene, hoping that the goddess would soon appear to him with her gleaming shield, her aegis. He did not have long to wait. He was contemplating images of the three Gorgons, set up when Medusa was beautiful, when suddenly he found himself gazing once more into the gray eyes of Athene. He quickly dropped to his knees in worship.

"Rise, Perseus," Athene commanded. "You understand the difficulties and the dangers you must overcome if you are to carry through your task?"

Perseus bowed his head in assent.

"But be not afraid. The gods look with approval on your enterprise," Athene told him. As she spoke, Hermes, the messenger of Olympus and patron of adventurers, swooped down upon his winged sandals.

"I have brought for you a sickle that nothing can break, blunt, or bend," said Hermes, handing the weapon to Perseus. "It was forged by Hephaistos himself at the request of Father Zeus."

While Hermes was telling Perseus how he was to decapitate Medusa with one swift cut of the sickle, Perseus was envying the winged sandals of the messenger of Olympus. Hermes smiled.

"You are wondering if I am going to lend you my winged sandals. No, that is not possible. What you must do now is search for the Stygian Nymphs in Arcadia. They dwell beside the dark pool of Styx before the river runs down into Tartarus."

"Why must I search for the Stygian Nymphs?" Perseus asked.

"Because they were charged by King Hades with the guardianship of another pair of winged sandals, of a magic bag that will hold the Gorgon's head, and, even more important, of the Cap of Darkness that makes its wearer invisible."

"If you succeed in persuading the Stygian Nymphs to help you," Athene said, "you must find out from them where the Graiae live."

"The Graiae?" Perseus asked.

"The three gray sisters of the same race as the three Gorgon sisters. They were born gray-headed and have only one tooth and one eye between them. Somehow you must think of a way to make them tell you how to find the Gorgons. And now here is my gift to help you in the task you have undertaken."

With these words Athene gave young Perseus her gleaming aegis.

"When you find the Gorgons be sure not to look directly at Medusa or you will be turned to stone. Strike with your sickle when you see yourself and her reflection in my aegis. And as soon as the head of

Hermes gave Perseus a sickle forged by Hephaistos

Medusa falls from her, pick it up without looking at it and put it in the bag you are given by the Stygian Nymphs. Farewell, Perseus. Fear not. The gods of Olympus wish you well."

A moment later Perseus was alone, contemplating again the images of the three Gorgon sisters. His next task was to reach Arcadia without his grandfather, King Akrisios, being aware that he was in the Peloponnese. We are not told how he managed this nor do we know how he was able to persuade the Stygian Nymphs to let him have the winged sandals, the magic bag, and the Cap of Darkness. Some say that the Stygian Nymphs had the faces of dogs and that Perseus was clever enough to make them believe he thought them beautiful. Anyway, whatever he did, the Nymphs let him have the winged sandals, the magic bag, and the Cap, and sped him on his way to the farthest west. Here the Titan Atlas stood bowed beneath the burden he had been condemned to bear after the gods of Olympus had defeated the desperate attempt of the Titans to destroy them. Zeus had sentenced Atlas to hold heaven and earth apart for ever.

Perseus told Atlas of his mission to cut off Medusa's head. He asked Atlas's help in finding the Graiae and learning from them how to reach the Gorgons. Atlas wanted Perseus to succeed; he longed to gaze at Medusa's head so that he would be turned to stone and be relieved of his endless burden.

"The Graiae sit beside a lake not far from here. But you will have to use cunning if you want to learn from them how to reach the Gorgons. You must wear the Cap of Darkness when you approach the lake. You must snatch the only tooth they have when they are passing it round, and refuse to give it back to them until you have the guidance you seek."

When Perseus saw the Graiae sitting beside the lake he was surprised that in spite of their great age they were still unwrinkled. He crept up behind them, invisible beneath the Cap of Darkness, and snatched their one tooth as it was being passed round.

The Graiae scolded Perseus furiously when he took off the Cap of Darkness and appeared to them, holding their tooth in his hand.

"I must know where I may find the Gorgons before I give you back your tooth," he told them.

The Graiae continued to scold him, but at last they muttered, "Give us back our tooth and you shall have what you want."

"Tell me where to find the Gorgons and you shall have your tooth," Perseus insisted.

The three sisters muttered away to one another until at last they said, "You must fly north and farther north, to the land of the Hyperboreans, and there you will find the three Gorgons. Now give us back our tooth."

Perseus gave the tooth back to the Graiae. Then he put on the Cap of Darkness and the winged sandals and

The three gray sisters

flew northward. As he flew north the air became colder. He had never before experienced extreme cold, and for the first time he began to wonder if he might fail in his task. As the wind swept round him in ever more chilly gusts he called upon the goddess Athene to give him the courage to endure.

At once confidence was restored to him. He flew on through cold torrents of rain over a stretch of treeless country. Then, among rocks that had the shape of mammoths and other wild beasts, he saw the three Gorgons on a hillock. He flew down and approached the hillock very carefully, because Athene had warned him to look not at Medusa but only at her reflection in the gleaming aegis. With one stroke of the sickle he severed Medusa's head and crammed it into the bag.

Then he flew southward. It was fortunate for him that he was still wearing the Cap of Darkness, because the two immortal sisters of Medusa spread their vampire wings and flew after him, their cries of fury audible above the wind. Although they could not see Perseus they were able to follow him by the clinking of the sickle against the aegis. When at last Perseus managed to stop the clinking he was able to escape from the two Gorgons, who were screaming revenge for the death of their mortal sister.

You can imagine the young Hero's relief when he left the Gorgons behind and could no longer hear those menacing shrieks and the swish of those vampire wings.

The sun was setting into the boundless ocean, when Perseus reached the domain of Atlas.

"Let me look into Medusa's eyes," said Atlas. "They will petrify me, and I shall be at rest. I shall set with my brother, the Sun."

So Perseus took Medusa's head from the bag. Atlas gazed upon it and was turned into Mount Atlas, which rises today in Morocco, where once the Titan held heaven and earth apart.

After resting for a night, Perseus flew across the Libyan desert. As he flew, some drops of blood fell from Medusa's head and became asps. Or so some people say. Others believe that it was the snakes in Medusa's hair that fell upon the desert and were the original asps. (One of the descendants of these asps, so the story goes, would one day sting to death Cleopatra of Egypt.)

Perseus continued on his way. He intended to take Medusa's head to Seriphos to keep his promise to King Polydektes. After that, he expected the goddess Athene to appear to him and tell him what next to do.

As he was flying above the coast of Philistia, near the city of Joppa, Perseus looked down and was amazed to see below him a young woman, naked except for a gem-studded necklace. She was standing on a rock projecting below a cliff, and, when Perseus flew closer, he saw that she was chained to the cliff. She was obviously terrified. She was also very beautiful. Perseus fell instantly in love with her, and determined to rescue her and make

Perseus fled from Medusa's vengeful sisters

her his wife. He could easily cut through the chains with his sickle. But first he decided to fly along the beach to where he could see a crowd of people standing by the water's edge; he wanted to know why this beautiful maiden had been chained to the cliff.

On the beach were Cepheus and Cassiopeia, the King and Queen of the land. King Cepheus told Perseus that the beautiful maiden was their daughter Andromeda and that she was to be the prey of a terrible sea-monster.

"Queen Cassiopeia claimed that she and Andromeda were more beautiful than the Nereids. The Nereids complained to King Poseidon, the mighty lord of the sea, who sent this horrible monster to ravage the land. We made sacrifices to Poseidon, but he did not heed them. Now the people have decided that the only way to appease him is to sacrifice my daughter."

"I will do battle with this sea-monster," Perseus vowed, "and if I overcome it I will cut your daughter's chain and bring her back to you safely. But I have one condition to make," he added.

"My treasury is open for you to take as much gold as you wish," Cepheus proclaimed grandly.

"I do not need your gold," Perseus declared. "I ask for your daughter's hand in marriage."

Unwillingly, Cepheus and Cassiopeia agreed. They had only just given their assent when loud cries of alarm arose along the beach. The savage and hideous monster was coming in from the sea.

Perseus flew above the monster and then, swooping down, slashed at it until its blood spurted. But he soon realized that he could not kill the monster with his sickle, only wound and enrage it. So he drew Medusa's head from the bag and, keeping his own eyes averted, held it before the wide-open, fire-breathing mouth. Immediately the monster was turned to stone.

Then Perseus flew down to sever the chains of the beautiful maiden with whom he had fallen so deeply in love. Cassiopeia wrapped Andromeda in a garment and, with a far from friendly glance at Perseus, bade her daughter return with her to the palace in Joppa. Andromeda looked back at the young Hero who had saved her life. In her eyes was the glow of a love for Perseus as deep as his for her.

Cepheus lingered to say that he supposed Perseus would also be coming to the palace. But he said it in such a disagreeable tone that the young Hero looked at him with sudden suspicion.

"You have not forgotten that you promised me your daughter's hand if I rescued her from the jaws of the sea-monster?"

"I have not forgotten," Cepheus replied, "but it would be as well if you came and stayed with us at our palace in order to let my people get to know you before you marry their princess."

"It must not be too long before our wedding. The goddess Athene awaits my return to Hellas."

The monster emerged from the sea

King Cepheus did not comment. He turned and walked away toward the palace with his attendants.

When Perseus was left alone on the beach, he stripped off his garments and prepared to bathe in the sea. He wanted to be sure that none of the monster's blood remained on his arms and neck. Before he plunged, he laid Medusa's head on a bed of seaweed, which immediately became a bed of coral.

Refreshed by his bathe, Perseus felt that he must show his gratitude to the gods for the help they had given him during his great adventure. He had emerged unharmed, with his task accomplished and the prospect of marrying the beautiful Andromeda happily before him. So he built three altars—to Zeus, Athene, and Hermes. To Zeus he sacrificed a bull, to Athene a cow, and to Hermes a calf. He watched the fumes rising from his triple sacrifice and was heartened to see how steadily the smoke rose toward the cloudless sky.

He was ready now to go to the royal palace in Joppa. He debated with himself for a moment or two whether to leave Medusa's head on the bed of coral or take it with him to the palace. He decided to leave it where it was. After all, anybody who tried to steal it would instantly be turned to stone.

When Perseus arrived at the palace, Cepheus and Cassiopeia quickly made it clear to him that they resented the prospect of his marrying their only daughter. Cassiopeia was particularly bitter. She knew that it was her vanity that had stirred the Nereids to anger and that it was she who would have been responsible for her daughter's ghastly death had it not been for Perseus.

Andromeda realized that her mother meant to do all she could to prevent her marriage to this young Hellene, whose fair head seemed so much fairer among the dark complexions all around her. While still a girl, Andromeda had been betrothed by her parents to a young man named Agenor. She was afraid that Agenor would now claim her as his bride and that the King, her father, might make her betrothal to Agenor an excuse for breaking his promise to Perseus.

"You must insist that our wedding takes place at once," Andromeda urged Perseus. "Do not heed any excuses my father makes for its postponement. If we delay, Agenor, who is the twin brother of mighty King Belos, will have time to gather an armed force and come to Joppa to carry me away from you. If that should happen, I would rather the terrible monster had taken me and devoured me."

"Nobody shall take you from me," Perseus avowed. "Is the slayer of the Gorgon Medusa to be robbed of her whom he loves by a Philistine? Never!"

So, in spite of all the delays that King Cepheus and Queen Cassiopeia contrived to bring about, a day for the wedding was named. But Cassiopeia had sent a messenger to Agenor to tell him of the date, in the hope that he would arrive in time to prevent the marriage.

Perseus washed away the monster's blood

So it happened that, in the middle of the ceremony, Agenor with many armed retainers burst into the palace. Perseus found himself surprised by formidable adversaries, with only his sword to defend himself against heavy odds. Fortunately, the gleaming shield of Athene was in the hall and he quickly seized it. Cassiopeia and her ladies-in-waiting tried to hustle the bride away. Andromeda wept and protested. Cassiopeia bade her daughter stop crying and be silent.

"Your golden-haired intruder from Hellas will be killed and your wedding feast will be for your marriage with Agenor, to whom you were betrothed by your parents while you were still a child."

Andromeda paid no attention to what her mother was saying. She gazed at her with loathing.

"I no longer look upon you and the King as my parents. You were willing to sacrifice me to appease the wrath of Poseidon, although it was you who aroused his wrath by boasting that you were more beautiful than the Nereids. You chained me naked by the shore to be devoured by that horrible sea-monster. I was saved by Perseus, and for the rest of the life I owe to him he shall be the master of that life."

"Then you will be giving your life to a corpse," Cassiopeia said with a cruel smile.

And indeed at that moment it looked as if the malice of Cassiopeia would be gratified and that her words would prove too sadly true.

Perseus had cut down several of his adversaries, but others kept assailing him, and he realized that however hard he fought he must inevitably be overcome by numbers. In his peril he called upon Athene.

"O goddess, have I accomplished the task in which you were my guiding light only to be conquered by these foul swarthy Philistines? Help me, divine Athene!"

He did not say these words aloud, but prayed silently. And instantly he knew that somehow he must reach Medusa's head on its bed of coral beside the shore. He broke away from his assailants and ran from the palace. He reached the head as Agenor's men came charging along the beach.

Perseus held up the head of Medusa when the first dozen or so of his enemies, their swords flashing in the sunshine, were almost upon him. A second later, and he was faced by a dozen or so petrified warriors, standing motionless, like statues, on the beach. Those behind drew hurriedly back to avoid Medusa's deadly stare. Agenor himself recognized that the gods were on the side of Perseus. He decided to give up all claims to the hand of Andromeda and to leave Joppa with his retainers.

The wedding feast that had been so roughly interrupted was resumed. Both King Cepheus and Queen Cassiopeia were now effusively polite to their son-in-law and begged him to stay in Joppa with his bride.

Perseus was not taken in by this change of attitude. He had no intention of remaining in Joppa. He was

Agenor's warriors were turned to stone

anxious to get home. He took advantage of the obvious desire of Cepheus to be on good terms with him by asking for a ship to take him back to Seriphos.

A ship and a crew of oarsmen were at once put at his disposal, and with Andromeda he bade farewell to Cepheus and Cassiopeia and left Joppa behind him for ever.

Remembering that Athene had bidden him to go to Samos before he set out on his quest for the head of Medusa, he put in at that island on the way to Seriphos. He was standing by the images of the three Gorgons, thinking how fantastic it was that he should be looking at them with the head of the only mortal one in a bag slung over his shoulder, when Hermes came swooping down from the sky to stand beside him.

"My sister, Athene, will be with you on Seriphos," said the messenger of the gods. "You will take with you the head of Medusa, but you will give me the Cap of Darkness and the winged sandals, and I will give them back to the Stygian Nymphs."

Perseus handed over the Cap of Darkness and the winged sandals, and Hermes flew away.

It was high time that Perseus returned to Seriphos. King Polydektes had never supposed for a moment that Perseus would succeed in his mad adventure. He had simply hoped that the silly young braggart would get into trouble and perhaps be killed.

No sooner had Perseus left Seriphos than Polydektes had pressed Danaë to marry him more insistently than ever. At last, wearied by the King's ceaseless attempts to win her hand in marriage, Danaë had taken refuge in the temple of Athene. Here she was safe from any violence Polydektes might attempt. He could not carry her off; indeed, he could not reach her to press her to marry him. What he could do, however, was to forbid any food to be taken into the temple.

So, when Perseus arrived back in Seriphos, he found that his mother was dying from hunger. He took her from the temple and put her into the care of Andromeda, who was delighted to be able to show in this way her love and gratitude to the young Hero who had rescued her and was now her beloved husband.

Diktys was glad indeed to see again the young Hero over whose boyhood he had presided and whose courage as a warrior and prowess as an athlete he had fostered.

"But you are only just in time," he told Perseus. "My brother was making it more and more difficult for me to get enough food to your mother to keep her alive."

Perseus was determined that the reign of Polydektes should come to an end. After the way he had disposed of his assailants at Joppa he had no reason to doubt his ability to overcome the King's supporters and he felt sure that the majority of the islanders would welcome Diktys as their ruler.

When Perseus reached the palace he found the courtiers enjoying a feast with their monarch. His entrance was greeted with jeers.

Andromeda took care of Danaë

"Well, my brave young man, so you have brought me Medusa's head as you promised. You will doubtless be showing it to me presently."

There was a burst of mocking laughter.

"Yes, I have brought you the head of Medusa as I promised," Perseus said coldly.

There was more laughter.

"Do you wish to see it?" the young Hero asked.

"We certainly do wish to see it," said Polydektes.

"We do indeed," his courtiers shouted obsequiously.

"When you see it, make the most of that instant, for it will be the very last moment of your lives."

As he spoke, Perseus took the head from the bag and held it in front of him. A moment later King Polydektes and his guests sat around the banqueting table in stony silence. They had all been petrified.

(You can still see today, on Seriphos, as I did more than fifty years ago, a semicircle of large stones that, legend has it, was all that was left of King Polydektes and his courtiers.)

As Perseus walked away from that petrified banquet the goddess Athene appeared.

"You have done well, Perseus," the goddess said. Now give me Medusa's head. I have a place for it. I will send back the bag to the Stygian Nymphs by the messenger of Olympus."

There are different legends about the way in which Athene made use of Medusa's head. The one most generally accepted is that she incorporated it in some way into her own aegis and made herself more invincible than ever. As for today, we still have a link with the legend of Medusa when we talk of somebody being "petrified by fear."

Perseus now decided that the time had come to go back to Argos, the famous city in which he had been born. He took his leave of the fisherman who had saved his life and the life of Danaë by bringing ashore the chest that had floated from Argolis to the Cyclades.

"You are now King Diktys and I know that you will rule Seriphos more wisely than your brother Polydektes. I shall never forget what I owe to you."

Somehow Perseus' grandfather King Akrisios had heard of his grandson's intention to come to Argos. By now the tale of the young Hero's exploits had reached Hellas. Akrisios, mindful of the prophecy that he would one day be killed by his grandson, left the city and took refuge with the King of the Pelasgians in Larissa, in what today is called Thessaly.

Akrisios need not have fled from Argos. Perseus had no desire to avenge his grandfather's cruelty and was determined to prove the oracle wrong.

Yet the prophecy had been all too true. The King of the Pelasgians held the funeral games for his father and asked Perseus to compete. Perseus could never resist displaying his athletic prowess. When it came to his turn to throw the discus he threw it with his usual skill, but a

Medusa's head petrified Polydektes' guests

sudden gust of wind caught it and changed its course. Among the spectators was Akrisios. The discus struck him on the head and killed him. The prophecy was fulfilled.

Perseus was distraught at shedding the blood of his grandfather, however unwittingly. He felt that if he continued to reign as King of Argos he would suffer misfortune. Proitos, the twin brother of Akrisios, had died and had been succeeded as King of Tiryns by his son Megapenthes. Perseus suggested, and it was agreed, that he and Megapenthes should exchange kingdoms.

So Perseus reigned in Tiryns and became the ancestor of many Hellenic Heroes. His son Perses went to Asia Minor and gave his name to the country called Persia, which is now known as Iran.

Perseus himself founded and built with the Cyclopes the city of Mycenae, which was to have an immortal future of military glory, grandeur, and tragedy. It was from Mycenae that Agamemnon led the Greeks against Troy. It was in Mycenae that Agamemnon was murdered by his wife Clytemnestra. It was called Mycenae because one day Perseus was feeling thirsty and he was looking for a spring of water. He found one beside a clump of fungi. The Greek word for fungus is "mykos." Today we still call the study of fungi "mycology," and today in Greece the most awe-inspiring relic of that faraway past is Mycenae. It is strange that something as short-lived as a fungus should have given its name to a city of enduring heroic fame.

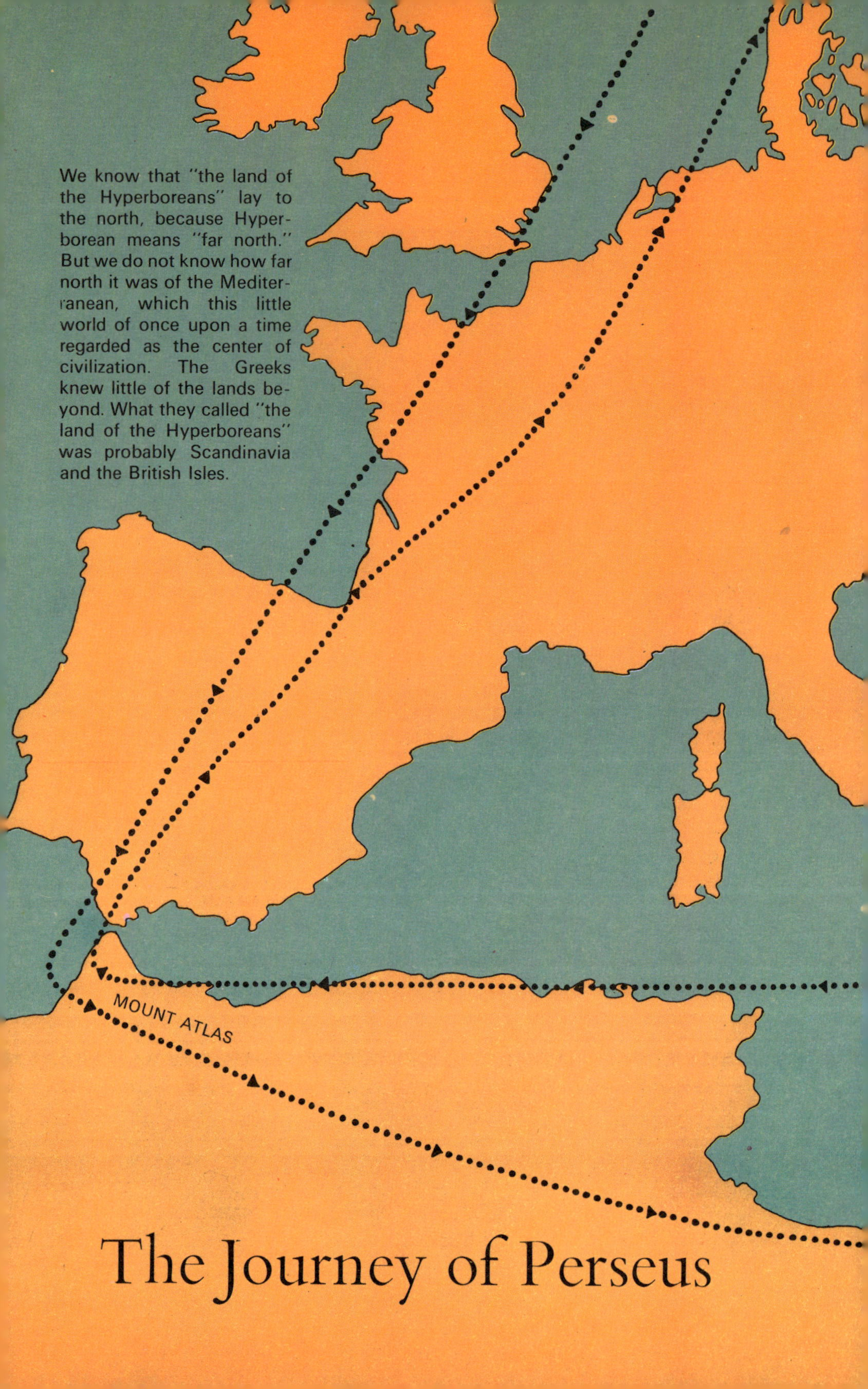

We know that "the land of the Hyperboreans" lay to the north, because Hyperborean means "far north." But we do not know how far north it was of the Mediterranean, which this little world of once upon a time regarded as the center of civilization. The Greeks knew little of the lands beyond. What they called "the land of the Hyperboreans" was probably Scandinavia and the British Isles.

The Journey of Perseus

HELLAS
THESSALY
Larissa
Mycenae
Argos
Tiryns
ARGOLIS
ARCADIA
PELOPONNESE
CYCLADES
SERIPHOS
SAMOS
ASIA MINOR
LYCIA
Joppa
PHILISTIA
LIBYAN DESERT

Jason

The Story of
JASON

GODS AND GODDESSES

IN THE STORY OF JASON

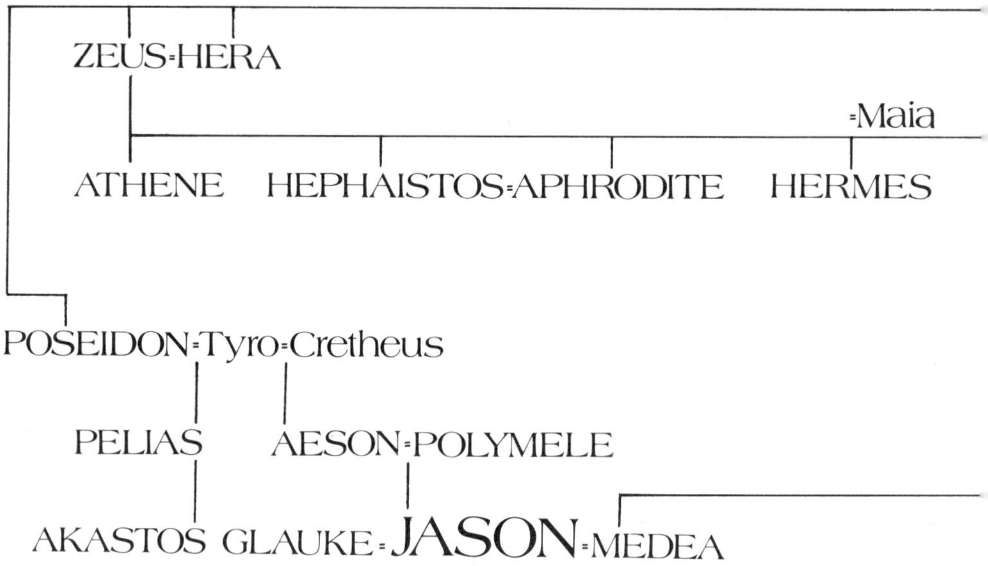

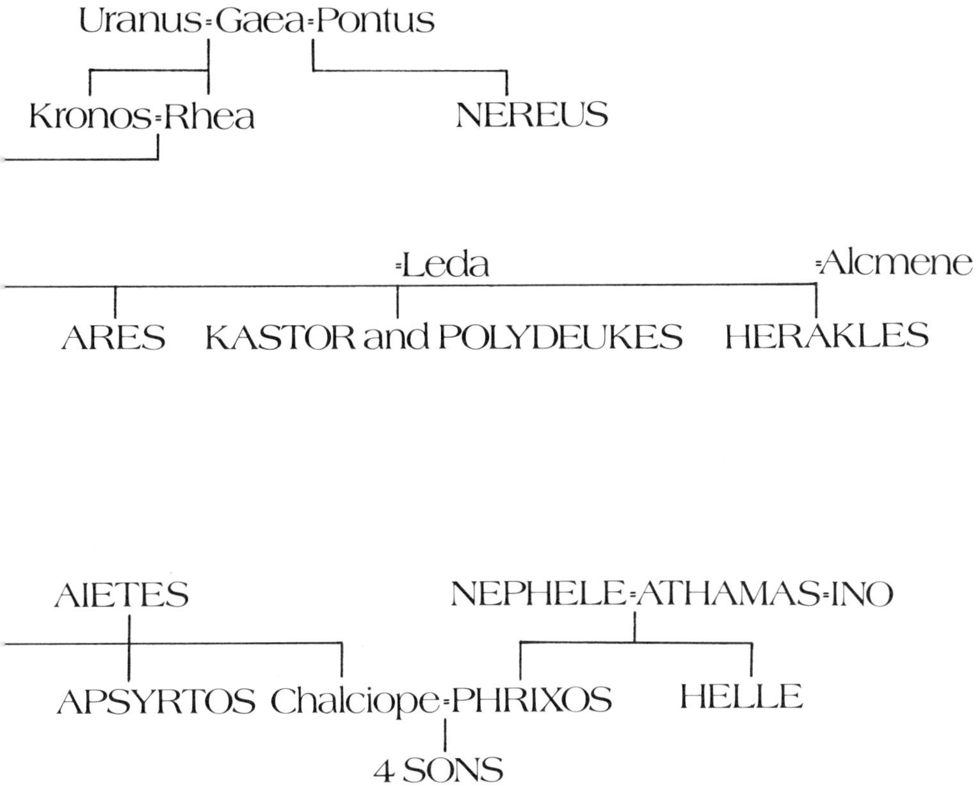

This family tree shows the gods and goddesses of ancient Greece, and the demigods and mortals related to them, whose lives are linked with that of Jason, the hero of this story of once upon a time. Those whose names are in capitals—for example, MEDEA and AESON—played a direct. part in Jason's adventures. Those whose names are not in capitals—such as Tyro, mother of PELIAS—take their places in the tree as links in the line of descent from Gaea, the Earth-mother. It was believed in that world of long ago that Gaea was created out of Chaos. She brought forth Uranus (Heaven) and Pontus (Sea), by both of whom she then had children. From her were descended all the other gods and goddesses of Greece.

Hermes and the golden ram

Jason

Once upon a time there was a King of Boeotia whose name was Athamas. He was married to a cloud-nymph called Nephele and they had a son, Phrixos, and a daughter, Helle. But Athamas was unhappy. His wife Nephele thought herself superior to him and she used to leave him from time to time to wander on Mount Olympus. In the end, Athamas grew tired of Nephele's wanderings and took a new wife, Ino. Ino was jealous of her step-children and wanted to rid herself of them.

At this time, King Athamas was worried because Boeotia had had a succession of bad harvests. He sent messengers to seek the advice of the Delphic Oracle. Ino saw her chance. She bribed the messengers to bring back a false report from the Oracle. They told Athamas that if he wanted to be sure of a good harvest he must sacrifice his son and daughter to Zeus. Athamas, shocked and unwilling, nonetheless felt obliged to obey the Oracle. Nephele, the children's mother, begged Hera, the Queen of Heaven, to prevent the sacrifice. Hera asked Zeus, who loathed all human sacrifices, to intervene.

To rescue Phrixos and Helle, Zeus sent Hermes, the messenger of the gods, and a winged ram that had a fleece of gold. Hermes and the ram arrived at the scene of sacrifice just as Athamas was raising the knife to cut his son's throat. Gratefully, Athamas put down the knife and Hermes bade both Phrixos and Helle mount upon the back of the ram with the golden fleece.

With the two young people upon its back the ram flew east toward Colchis, on the eastern shores of the Black Sea. As it was crossing the strait of water that divides Europe from Asia, Helle grew dizzy and fell from the ram's back into the water below. In her honor, we now call the strait into which she fell "the Hellespont."

Phrixos flew on alone to Colchis, where he sacrificed the winged ram to Zeus. The golden fleece he hung in a temple of Ares, the god of war. This temple stood in the heart of a grove and was guarded day and night by a dragon. Aietes, King of Colchis, was proud to have the golden fleece in his country and he gave one of his daughters to Phrixos in marriage. In due course, after fathering four sons, Phrixos died. In accordance with the custom of the Colchians, his body was not buried but hung in an ox hide on the top of a tall willow tree, where the vultures would leave only his bones.

Afterward, the ghost of Phrixos began to haunt King Pelias of Iolkos in Thessaly. The ghost moaned that it could not gain entrance to the Underworld of Tartarus until its bones had had proper burial. It urged King Pelias to send an expedition to bury the bones and to bring the golden fleece back to Hellas. Until this were done, it warned, the land of Iolkos would never prosper.

At about this time, King Pelias, who had usurped the throne of Iolkos from his step-brother Aeson, was warned by an oracle that he would be slain one day by a kinsman wearing only one sandal. So this wicked king gave a banquet, at which he massacred all those connected with his house who were over twenty years old. Aeson he spared and kept a prisoner in his palace.

Soon after this, Polymele, the wife of Aeson, had a baby son. Afraid that Pelias would kill the baby, Polymele and her handmaidens wept and mourned, pretending that the baby had been stillborn. Then they smuggled the baby boy away to Mount Pelion and put him in the care of the noble centaur Cheiron. The centaurs had the heads and shoulders of men and the bodies of horses; most of them were savage, but Cheiron was a noble exception. In his cave high up on Mount Pelion he was the tutor of more famous Heroes than any tutor who has ever lived.

Polymele had named her son Diomedes, but Cheiron changed the baby's name to Jason, and as Jason he was ever afterward known.

When Jason was approaching his twentieth birthday, the wise centaur decided that the time had come for him to claim his rightful place in the kingdom of Iolkos. He was, after all, the true heir to the throne of Iolkos. Pelias was growing old, the kingship was becoming a burden to him, and it was unlikely that he would dare now to deny his step-nephew's rights. And the people of Iolkos would probably welcome a younger monarch.

Helle fell from the ram's back

So Jason left the cave where he had spent such a happy boyhood with other young Heroes, some of whom would be the fathers of Heroes even more famous than their sires. He was sad for a while as he trudged toward Iolkos, his only weapon a spear whose staff he had cut from one of the famous ash trees of Mount Pelion. At last he came to a raging torrent, on the opposite bank of which an old crone was standing.

"Help me, help me, young sir! Help a poor old woman to cross!"

Jason remembered Cheiron's injunction always to help the aged or the infirm. Without a moment's hesitation he plunged in, waded to the opposite bank, and hoisted the old woman onto his back. As he fought his way back through the water, his feet slithered in the mud, and one of his sandals came off and was carried away.

"Well, there you are," he panted, lifting the old woman down from his back. "I hope you will have no more rivers to cross on your way home."

Imagine his surprise when he heard a voice of utter beauty reply,

"There will be no torrent for me to cross on Olympus."

Turning quickly, he saw, instead of the aged crone he had carried on his back, a tall young woman clothed in gleaming white. She had the largest and loveliest eyes he had ever beheld. Instinctively Jason knew that this figure of radiant womanhood was a goddess, no less a goddess than Queen Hera herself. He knelt down in worship.

"Rise, young Hero," the goddess bade him. "I am henceforth your friend. I am much displeased with your uncle Pelias. It is natural for him to sacrifice to his father Poseidon, the ruler of the sea, but that is no excuse for his failure for some years now to offer any sacrifice to me."

With these words the goddess vanished.

This meeting with the Queen of Heaven filled Jason with serene confidence. He walked briskly on to Iolkos. When he arrived, he found that King Pelias had again been offering sacrifices to Poseidon and was now giving a great banquet on the seashore to the kings and princes who had attended.

When Pelias saw the stranger wearing only one sandal, he remembered the oracle's warning.

"Who are you?" he demanded fearfully.

"I am Diomedes, son of Aeson, now called Jason." There were shouts of welcome from the assembled guests. Many of them were kinsmen of the young Hero, so Pelias did not dare call his men-at-arms to seize Jason.

"What would you do, young man, if you had been told by an oracle that a kinsman with one sandal would kill you?" he demanded fiercely.

Hera put the reply into Jason's mouth:

"I would bid him go to Colchis, bury the bones of Phrixos, and bring back to Hellas the Golden Fleece."

Pelias saw immediately that here was his chance to free himself from the ghost of Phrixos. He bade Jason fulfill his words with actions. Jason accepted the challenge,

Jason carried the hag across the torrent

full of confidence and never for a moment thinking he could fail in the task he had set himself.

Jason persuaded Argos the Thespian to design and build for him a larger longboat than had ever before been built in Hellas. It was to be called the *Argo*. There were to be fifty oarsmen. Jason sent heralds all over Hellas calling for volunteers from the Heroes to man the *Argo*. So many of these young Heroes arrived at Iolkos that Jason had to turn away most of them when he picked the fifty oarsmen who were to become famous as the Argonauts. One of those he picked was Akastos, son of Pelias.

Jason felt more than ever sure that the Olympians approved of the expedition when Athene brought to him a beam cut from the sacred grove of oaks around the oracle of Zeus at Dodona, the most revered oracle in Hellas. He had the sacred beam fixed in the prow of the *Argo*, whose hull was built of timbers from Mount Pelion.

In due course, the Argonauts launched the *Argo* from Pagasae, the port of Iolkos. Then, a few days before they were due to sail, Herakles arrived. He had just completed his Fourth Labor, the capture of the Erymanthian Boar, and felt in need of a different adventure before undertaking his remaining tasks. The Argonauts were so excited by the arrival of the strongest man on earth that they unanimously voted him commander of the expedition. Jason was willing to hand over his command, but Herakles refused it. He would share a bench with Jason as an oarsman, but he would not take command of the *Argo*.

The Argonauts dined together on the evening before they sailed. One of their number sang, and played his lyre, to entertain them. This was Orpheus himself, who entranced his companion Heroes that night before they set out on the greatest voyage the world had yet known.

The first stop for food and water was to be the island of Lemnos. When the *Argo* approached the port of Myrine on the west side of the island, the Argonauts were astonished to see crowds of armed women on the shore, apparently determined to resist their landing.

Lemnos was the haunt on earth of Hephaistos, who would sometimes descend to the island from his great smithy on Olympus to work at his mechanical marvels. Aphrodite, his wife, had thought that the women of Lemnos did not pay her due reverence, and to punish them she had afflicted them with foul breath. As a result, Lemnian husbands had found their wives so repulsive that they went on long fishing cruises to Thrace and spent most of their time making love to Thracian girls. Finally, the Lemnian women had become so incensed by their husbands' neglect that one night they murdered them all; not a single male now existed on the island.

Jason sent a herald to explain why the Argonauts had put in at Myrine. Reassured, Hypsipyle, the Queen of the island, provided wine and food for the voyagers. She became much attracted to Jason, and tried to persuade him to marry her and settle in Lemnos. Jason told her that when he had brought back the Golden Fleece he

The women of Lemnos

might return to marry her. But Aphrodite had by now taken her unpleasant curse from the Lemnian women, and he and the other Argonauts were in no hurry to leave the island. Only Herakles remained on board the *Argo*. One night, tired of being left to guard the ship with only his young squire, Hylas, for company, he went ashore and, banging at every door with his great club, shouted angrily at the Argonauts that they must come back to the ship at once. In vain the Lemnians tried to make them stay; Herakles, when angry, was not to be disobeyed.

So at dawn next morning the *Argo* sailed for Samothrace, which rises from the sea like a huge triangle of rock. Orpheus was anxious that the Argonauts should be initiated into the Sacred Mysteries that belonged to the island. So they disembarked to partake in the rites of Samothrace and then set sail for the Hellespont.

The Hellespont was guarded by the city of Troy, whose King, Laomedon, tried to prevent any Hellenic ship from entering its waters. The Argonauts did not reach the mouth of the Hellespont until it was dark. Then, keeping as close as possible to the Thracian coast, on the opposite shore to Troy, they managed to reach the Sea of Marmara without being seen.

The next port of call of the *Argo* was a rocky peninsula called Arktonesos, or Bear Island. Here King Kyzikos was celebrating his marriage feast, to which he invited the Argonauts. The four Argonauts left to guard the ship were attacked by some gigantic six-handed men who were armed with clubs and stones, but the guards beat them off. These giants lived high up in the heart of Arktonesos.

Next day King Kyzikos bade the Argonauts a warm farewell and wished them a happy ending for their daring enterprise. The weather seemed fair and the *Argo* sailed on eastward toward the Bosporus. Suddenly, as can still happen in these waters today, a fierce northeast gale blew up. The oarsmen struggled against it until they began to tire. Then Tiphys the helmsman decided to turn back, intending to shelter on the west side of Bear Island until the gale died down. But in the darkness he steered to the *east* side and the *Argo* had to be hurriedly beached to avoid being wrecked. Suddenly, out of the windswept darkness, came armed men to attack the Argonauts. There was a fierce battle, in which several of the enemy were killed before the rest turned and fled. Jason called for a lamp to see who these unexpected assailants were and, to his horrified amazement, looked down at the dead body of the kindly King Kyzikos, whom he himself had slain. The King had supposed that the Argonauts were marauding pirates and had led his men-at-arms to drive them off.

The Argonauts remained on Bear Island to take part in the funeral games for King Kyzikos. Their sorrow was deepened by the news that Kleite, the beautiful young bride of the kindly, generous, and hospitable King, had hanged herself.

It may have been to raise the spirits of the Argonauts that, when at last the weather looked set fair and they

Six-armed giants attacked the *Argo*

were able to continue the voyage, Herakles proposed a contest of endurance, to see which of the Argonauts could outrow the others. Only Tiphys and Orpheus were excluded from this contest, the former because he had to steer the *Argo* and the latter because he had to stave off the fatigue of the oarsmen with his sublime music.

One by one the competitors fell back from the benches exhausted, until at last only four were still rowing—Herakles, Jason, and the Heavenly Twins—Kastor, the champion horse-tamer of Hellas, and Polydeukes, the champion boxer. Then the Twins gave up; Herakles and Jason kept on. Finally, as the *Argo* approached the mouth of a river in Mysia, Jason fainted. A moment later the oar of Herakles broke with a loud crack. Half of it was carried out to sea. Herakles himself fell backward from his bench. He was so furious that for a moment it looked as if he were going to lay the other half of his oar about the shoulders of his companions. They hurriedly manned their oars and started to row again. Soon they managed to beach the *Argo* beside the bank of the river.

The people of Mysia received the Argonauts warmly and gave them food, which by now they badly needed. Herakles, who was still angry about his broken oar, did not eat anything but went off into the woods to find a tree from which he could cut himself a new oar. He uprooted a great pine and dragged it back to the camp.

He called for his young squire Hylas to come and help him, but Hylas did not answer. The other Argonauts told

Herakles that, an hour before, the youth had gone to fetch water from a nearby spring, known as the Spring of Pegae. Herakles at once hastened to the spring, shouting for Hylas. On his way he met Polyphemus, another Argonaut, who told him that there was no sign of Hylas at the spring—only the pitcher he had carried to fetch the water. All that night, Herakles and Polyphemus called out for Hylas; but there was no answer. There never would be any answer. The water-nymphs of Pegae had been so charmed by the beauty of Hylas that they had pulled him down to a grotto beneath the water, where they kept him to be their playmate.

When dawn came, Herakles and Polyphemus were still searching. But an offshore breeze had sprung up and Tiphys called on the Argonauts to get aboard quickly and make the most of it. They were naturally unwilling to sail without Herakles and Polyphemus, but Glaukos, the herald of the sea god Nereus, rose from the sea, clutched the *Argo*'s keel, and announced:

"Herakles has to perform his next Labor. Polyphemus is destined to found a city in Mysia. A water-nymph will take Hylas for her husband, and he will be happy."

On their way through the Sea of Marmara the Argonauts called at the island of Bebrykos for food and water. The island was ruled by an aggressive and haughty young King called Amykos. It was his habit to challenge strangers who landed on Bebrykos to a boxing match and, if they declined, to fling them over a cliff into the sea.

Hylas and the water-nymphs

When he challenged the Argonauts, Polydeukes, the champion boxer of the Olympic Games, unhesitatingly stepped forward. After a long and fiercely contested bout, he killed the arrogant young King with a ferocious blow on the temple. The Argonauts were attacked by the Bebrykians, but defeated them and sacked the royal palace. Jason then sacrificed twenty red bulls to Poseidon, the father of Amykos. He did not want to incur Poseidon's hostility on his way across the Black Sea.

After other adventures, the Argonauts reached Salmydessus, a small city in Eastern Thrace, close to where the city of Constantinople stands today. Phineus, the blind King of Salmydessus, received them hospitably. Phineus was so accurate and far-seeing a prophet, that it was said that the gods had blinded him out of envy.

What was worrying Phineus now, much more than his blindness, was the malice of two horrible creatures called Harpies. They were winged and feathered women with ugly faces who, as soon as any food was laid out before the King, would fly down onto the table and befoul what they did not gobble up.

When King Phineus invited the Argonauts to a banquet, down flew the two Harpies. And up stood two of the Argonauts, Zetes and Kalais, the winged sons of Boreas, the North Wind. Drawing their swords, they attacked the Harpies, who fled. Zetes and Kalais pursued them, until, somewhere in Greece, they promised to give up their foul habits and cease molesting Phineus.

King Phineus, grateful to the Argonauts for ridding him of these foul pests, offered to give them whatever help he could. The first problem was how the *Argo* was to pass between two clashing rocks that guarded the entrance to the Black Sea from the Bosporus. Whenever a ship tried to sail between them, the rocks drove together and crushed it. On Phineus's advice a dove was sent flying in front of the *Argo*. The rocks clashed, but they cut off only some of the dove's tail feathers. The oarsmen rowed with all their might to get through before the rocks clashed again and just managed to do so with some small damage to the decorations of the *Argo's* stern.

Before the Argonauts embarked from Salmydessus, King Phineus had advised Jason to trust in Aphrodite's help once he reached Colchis. Phineus knew that Hera and Athene had asked Aphrodite to help Jason.

Once past the clashing rocks, the Argonauts sailed along the southern coast of the Black Sea. Soon they had to take shelter in the lee of an islet, where they picked up four mariners clinging to a piece of wreckage. These four shipwrecked mariners turned out to be the four sons of Phrixos, who had come from Aia, the capital city of their grandfather Aietes, King of Colchis.

Jason persuaded the sons of Phrixos to return to Colchis in the *Argo* so that they might bury the bones of their father. The other Argonauts welcomed the four new oars; they were under strength by now and their helmsman Tiphys had just died.

The *Argo* escaped the clashing rocks

The *Argo* sailed on eastward until the awe-inspiring mountains of the Caucasus seemed to cast a shadow on its prow. Coming to the mouth of a great river, the Phasis, the Argonauts rowed on until they reached a suitable backwater where they went ashore to decide on the best way to obtain the Golden Fleece. It was finally decided that Jason with the four sons of Phrixos should go to Aia and ask the King of Colchis to give them the Fleece. However, before they set out, Jason told the four sons to bury the bones of their father so that his unhappy ghost might descend to Tartarus across the Styx and reach the Elysian Fields. Beside the River Phasis was the grove of great willow trees, in the branches of which the bones of all the dead male Colchians were hung; only the females were buried. The sons of Phrixos took down the ox hide in which their father's body had been wrapped. Then they buried the bones with a piece of silver to pay Charon, the ferryman of Styx, to take them across the menacing river.

Then Jason set out with the four grandsons of King Aietes to visit the King in his palace. Princess Medea, the King's youngest daughter by his first wife, was present when Jason was shown into the royal audience chamber. She was dark and beautiful with a kind of unearthly fascination. She was a priestess of Hecate, the witch-goddess of the Underworld.

When Jason asked Aietes for the Golden Fleece, and offered in return the services of the Argonauts against the

King's enemies, Aietes told him contemptuously to be gone before he summoned his warriors to put Jason and his band of Argonauts to death.

"And as for you," he growled at his four grandsons, "you be gone, too. You know you had no right to break the laws of Colchis by burying your father's bones. You are banished for ever from my realm."

It was while Aietes was making these threats that Aphrodite came to the rescue of Jason as she had promised Hera and Athene that she would. With the present of a golden ball, she bribed her mischievous son Eros to shoot one of his arrows into Medea's heart, and in that instant Medea fell passionately in love with Jason.

"Why do you speak so harshly to this young Hero who saved the lives of your grandchildren? Why do you not set him a difficult task and, if he is successful in performing it, let him take the Golden Fleece back to Hellas?"

"I will set him a task, my daughter," the King replied with a savage grin. "Let him yoke my two fire-breathing bulls, and then let him plow a field and sow it with these dragon's teeth."

As he said this the King tossed a small bag at Jason's feet. Then he strode angrily out of the hall. Jason felt sure that he would never be able to accomplish the task. But when the four sons of Phrixos had left them together, Medea clasped him by the hand.

"If I succeed in giving you the Golden Fleece, swear by all the gods of Olympus that you will marry me and that

Medea fell instantly in love with Jason

you will remain faithful to me for the rest of your life?"

It is doubtful whether Jason ever really fell in love with Medea, but his heart was set on carrying back the Golden Fleece to Hellas as he had promised and there is no doubt that he did take that solemn oath.

"And now," said Medea, "you must set about your task. Before you try to yoke the fierce, fire-breathing bulls, rub yourself all over with this lotion. It is made from a crocus that sprang from the drops of blood shed by Prometheus when the eagle was tearing at his liver. It will protect you from the fiery breath of the bulls."

Jason went back to the *Argo* and ordered the Argonauts to row it to within a few miles of Aia. He told his companions of the tasks set him by King Aietes.

"If I succeed," he told them, "we shall take back with us to Hellas the Golden Fleece."

Next morning, after rubbing himself all over with the lotion given to him by Medea, Jason set out on his attempt to yoke the fire-breathing bulls. He had a desperate fight, but the lotion made him invulnerable to their fiery breath and he succeeded in yoking them.

After Jason had yoked the bulls, he plowed a large field and scattered the dragon's teeth over it. He was amazed to see an armed warrior spring from every tooth. For a moment or two he was at a loss, so he hid himself behind a pile of rocks while making up his mind what to do next. It was either Hera or Athene who inspired him to fling stones at the warriors. They started to accuse each other of throwing stones and soon they were all fighting fiercely among themselves until not one was left alive. You can imagine Jason's relief and also his joy at being able to go to King Aietes with his tasks fulfilled.

The King was furious.

"Give you the Golden Fleece!" he shouted. "Never! It must have been the witchery of that daughter of mine that helped you. She will not be able to help you any more. If you and your crew are not out of my realm by dawn my army will put you to the sword."

Jason left the palace and began to make his way back to the *Argo*. He was full of gloom, convinced that he had failed in his mission. But Medea caught his arm and whispered to him.

"Do not despair. I shall come at midnight to take you to the Golden Fleece."

When he reached the *Argo*, Jason summoned the Argonauts to a council of war and told them of the King's threat. A few of them wanted to weigh anchor and row down the river to the sea, but the majority voted to remain in the river and defy King Aietes and his Colchians.

Just before midnight Medea came to the *Argo* as she had promised. She led Jason and three or four of the Argonauts to a dark grove of holm-oaks, in the middle of which was the temple of Ares, the god of war. There, hanging from a pillar, was the Golden Fleece. To reach the Fleece, however, would be no easy task, for curled around the pillar was a huge dragon, which never slept.

Jason tamed the fire-breathing bulls

How Medea managed to get near enough to the dragon to sprinkle some opiate upon its eyes and send it to sleep we do not know. Presumably, as a priestess of the witch-goddess Hecate, she cast a secret spell. While the accompanying Argonauts held back the priests of Ares, Jason quickly unhooked the precious fleece. Then they all hurried back with it to the *Argo*. By the time they reached the ship, the priests of Ares had spread the news of the violation of their temple and before the Argonauts could weigh anchor they had a tough battle with the Colchian palace guards. Several Argonauts were wounded, includ- Jason, but only one, Iphitos of Mycenae, was killed.

Medea was able to cure the wounds of the Argonauts with her medicinal herbs and, although undermanned, they were able to reach the open sea without the Colchian galleys catching them. The reason why the galleys were unable to catch up with them is grim indeed. When Medea went on board the *Argo* she took with her Apsyrtos, the young son of King Aietes by his second marriage. To delay the Colchian galleys she killed her young half-brother and cut his body into fragments. These fragments she threw overboard into the river and, by the time the Colchian galleys had collected them, the *Argo* was back into the Black Sea.

Jason was shocked by Medea's ruthless deed. However, he owed to her the capture of the Golden Fleece and he had sworn by the Olympian gods to marry her and be faithful to her for the rest of his life. He allowed himself to forget that the Golden Fleece was still in his possession because a young life had been sacrificed to keep it.

So, at last, the Argonauts set out on their return journey to Thessaly. But when they reached the mouth of the Danube, on the western side of the Black Sea, Medea, advised by an oracle not to continue the journey until she had been cleansed of the death of Apsyrtos, begged Jason to take her overland to Illyria. Once there, she could go to the island of her aunt, the enchantress Circe, and be purified by her of shedding innocent blood.

Jason ordered the Argonauts to sail on with the Golden Fleece through the Bosporus, to reach the Aegean Sea, and sail on around the south of Hellas to find Medea and himself on Drepane.

Rather against her will, because she knew it would make her brother angry, Circe purified her niece. Perhaps Hecate the witch-goddess told her to purify her priestess Medea. After the purification, Medea and Jason left Circe's island and came to Drepane, where they were hospitably received by King Alcinous and Queen Arete. To Jason's joy the *Argo* had arrived safely with the Golden Fleece and was now beached. The Argonauts, glad to be so near home, were enjoying themselves on Drepane, but they were a little too soon in congratulating themselves on their good fortune. At dusk of the day on which Jason and Medea reached Drepane, the Colchian Fleet arrived and the Admiral sent a herald to demand the return of Medea and the Golden Fleece.

Jason and Medea

Queen Arete, who had been fascinated by Medea, urged King Alcinous to bid the Admiral return at noon next day to receive his answer. When the King retired to rest that night the Queen kept him awake with tales of the cruelty of kings to their daughters. She gave him one instance after another, and was particularly eloquent on the subject of King Akrisios's cruelty to his beautiful daughter Danaë, the mother of Perseus.

"And think what the Heroes of today would have lost as a noble example if Perseus had not been allowed to live."

King Alcinous said at last:

"If Medea is not married to Jason I shall have to hand her over to be taken back to King Aietes, but if they are married I shall refuse to hand her over."

As soon as Alcinous was fast asleep, Arete sent some of her handmaidens to find Medea.

"You must wed Jason tonight," she told her. "Celebrate your wedding feast in the great cave on the islet where the *Argo* is beached. I will send twelve of my handmaidens to help with the banquet and prepare the bridal couch."

It was dawn before Jason and Medea retired to their bridal couch, over which was spread the Golden Fleece. At noon of that happy day King Alcinous kept the promise he had made to his queen and refused to hand over either Medea or the Golden Fleece when the Colchian Admiral came to press his demands.

The Admiral was so frightened by the prospect of facing the wrath of King Aietes if he returned to Aia without either Medea or the Golden Fleece that he asked if he might remain and settle in Drepane. All the Colchian sailors were so much pleased with the beauty and the climate of this corner of the world that many of them settled there; others went farther up the Adriatic Sea and founded the city of Pola.

You can imagine with what energy the Argonauts bent to their oars as, helped by light Zephyrs from the west, the *Argo* came nearer and nearer to Cape Malea. The Argonauts would soon be seeing the olives of home and could rejoice that they were bringing back with them the Golden Fleece, rescued from barbarian Colchians after so many dangers survived, so many hazards overcome. But dangers and hazards still remained. Instead of rounding Cape Malea, the *Argo* was driven far back westward by a furious southeast wind, which today we call a sirocco.

Rather than be driven too far west, Jason set the *Argo*'s sail to take them up into the Tyrrhenian Sea along the western side of Italy. On the way the Argonauts had to pass the island of the Sirens. The Sirens were bird-women who had once been foolishly bold enough to challenge the Muses to a contest of music; they had been disgraced and deprived of their wings. Yet they still had voices so entrancing that sailors used to jump overboard and swim to the island to find them. The island was scattered with the bones of these bewitched mariners.

The island of the sirens

As the *Argo* drew near, Jason begged Orpheus to play his lyre as only he could play; his melodies were so beautiful that the Argonauts listened to him rather than to the Sirens. Nevertheless, one of them, Butes, did jump overboard and would have swum ashore to his death had not Aphrodite carried him off to a mountain in Sicily in order to make Adonis jealous.

There are various accounts of what the Argonauts did and where they went before at last they managed to sail around Cape Malea and could feel that they were nearly home. There were still many delays; the ship was continuously being driven back by those fierce summer gales of Boreas. But at last, on a serene October afternoon, the *Argo* anchored off the beach at Pagasae from which its voyage had begun.

There was nobody in sight except an elderly fisherman attending to his nets, who was astonished by the arrival of the *Argo*. He told the Argonauts that for two years or more it had been thought that the ship was lost. He went on to tell how the wicked King Pelias, now an old man, had killed Jason's father and mother.

Determined to avenge his parents' death, Jason summoned a council of war at which he called upon his fellow Argonauts to attack Iolkos. Akastos maintained that he could hardly be expected to attack his father and that in any case Iolkos was much too strong for them to hope to capture it. The other Argonauts, who were probably very anxious to get back to their various homes all over Hellas, argued that Akastos was right. However, they promised to collect together as many warriors as they could and come back to help Jason.

It was then that Medea spoke.

"I will capture Iolkos for you," she declared. "Take the *Argo* and beach it on some wooded shore within sight of the city. Hide yourselves until you see a torch flash from the palace roof. The city gates will then be open."

Medea had such an air of complete self-confidence that the Argonauts obeyed her commands. On one of the islands of the Cyclades, where the *Argo* had managed to shelter from Boreas, Medea had found an image of the goddess Artemis. She dressed in fantastic array twelve handmaidens whom Queen Arete had given her as a wedding gift and told them to take turns in carrying the image to the city gates. Turning herself into what seemed a very old woman, she led the way. When they reached the city gates at midnight Medea screamed, and all twelve handmaidens screamed with her, that the goddess Artemis had flown in a chariot drawn by winged serpents to bring good fortune to Iolkos. The guards opened the city gates and Medea with her handmaidens went screaming through the city, the inhabitants waking up and becoming as excited as they were.

Old King Pelias himself woke up also and when he heard that Medea was a messenger of Artemis he was a little nervous, especially when she told him that she had been sent by the goddess to make him young again. He

Maidens carried the image of Artemis

did not want to make an enemy of another goddess as he had of Hera. He questioned Medea cautiously:

"But if you can make me young," he asked, "why do you not make yourself young?"

Pelias was told to close his eyes; when he opened them there was Medea, young and dark and beautiful.

"And how will you make me young?" the old King asked in astonishment.

Then Medea killed and cut up an old ram and boiled the pieces in a pot, after which by sleight of hand she produced a lamb that she had concealed in the image of Artemis.

No doubt it was the magic of Medea's eyes that made Pelias tell his three daughters to cut him up. The eldest refused, but the other two cut their father up and put the pieces in a pot.

Medea told them to bring the boiling pot out on the palace roof and invoke the Moon goddess. The Argonauts saw the torchlight on the palace roof and came charging into the city.

Jason was so much shocked by the way his uncle had been destroyed that he resigned his claim to the throne of Iolkos, and went off to Thebes with the Golden Fleece. He placed it in a temple he built and dedicated to Zeus on the spot where the Golden Ram had flown away with Phrixos and Helle.

Medea now heard that her father Aietes had died of rage when he received the news about the failure of the Colchian fleet to capture his daughter and the Golden

Fleece. Now Aietes had been King of Corinth before he went to Colchis. He had left a regent behind, but the throne had been seized by a usurper who called himself Korinthos.

Medea, as the only surviving child of Aietes, considered herself the heiress to Corinth when she was told of her father's death. She persuaded Jason to take her to Corinth in the *Argo*, which Jason beached on the isthmus and dedicated to Poseidon. King Korinthos made Medea and Jason welcome. After they had been his guests for some time, Korinthos died suddenly and the Corinthians acclaimed Jason as their King.

For ten years he and Medea lived happily in Corinth with their children. Then Jason, after a visit to King Kreon of Thebes, fell in love with the King's daughter Glauke. Back in Corinth he suddenly accused Medea of poisoning Korinthos and told her they must be divorced. Medea admitted the poisoning, but reminded Jason that he had become King of Corinth as a result.

"You swore by all the gods of Olympus that you would be faithful to me for life."

Jason argued that such an oath was invalid because he had been compelled to take it in order to escape from Colchis with the Golden Fleece. Medea pretended to yield, but she was determined to be revenged. So she sent to Glauke a wedding present of a golden crown and a white bridal gown, which she had smeared with her deadly herbs. Suddenly Glauke's white robe burst into

Jason was abandoned by the gods

flames and the palace in Thebes, full of wedding guests, caught fire. Kreon tried to save his daughter but was burned with her. Many wedding guests were also burned to death and Jason only managed to escape by leaping from a high window.

And now he who had been loved by the Olympians was abandoned by them. The Corinthians dethroned him. Medea fled in her winged chariot to Athens, where King Aegeus married her. Some years later she fled again in that magic chariot when she failed to poison Theseus, after the young Hero had revealed himself to his father. She would live on to become almost as famous for her powers of sorcery as her aunt, Circe.

Alas, Jason was less fortunate; his ingratitude to Medea was bitterly punished. He wandered about from city to city in Hellas and was nowhere made welcome. At last, in a melancholy middle age, with the prospect of a lonely and miserable decline before him, he came to the isthmus and sat beside the *Argo*. He sat under the prow thinking sadly of all those brave adventures of once upon a time and of all those Heroes he had once led and who now despised him. What was the use of living any longer? He decided to hang himself from the prow of his beloved *Argo*. And, at last, the Olympians had pity on him. The prow that contained the sacred beam, given to Jason by Athene, fell upon him and killed him. Zeus took the stern of the famous ship into the sky, where it became the constellation *Argo*.

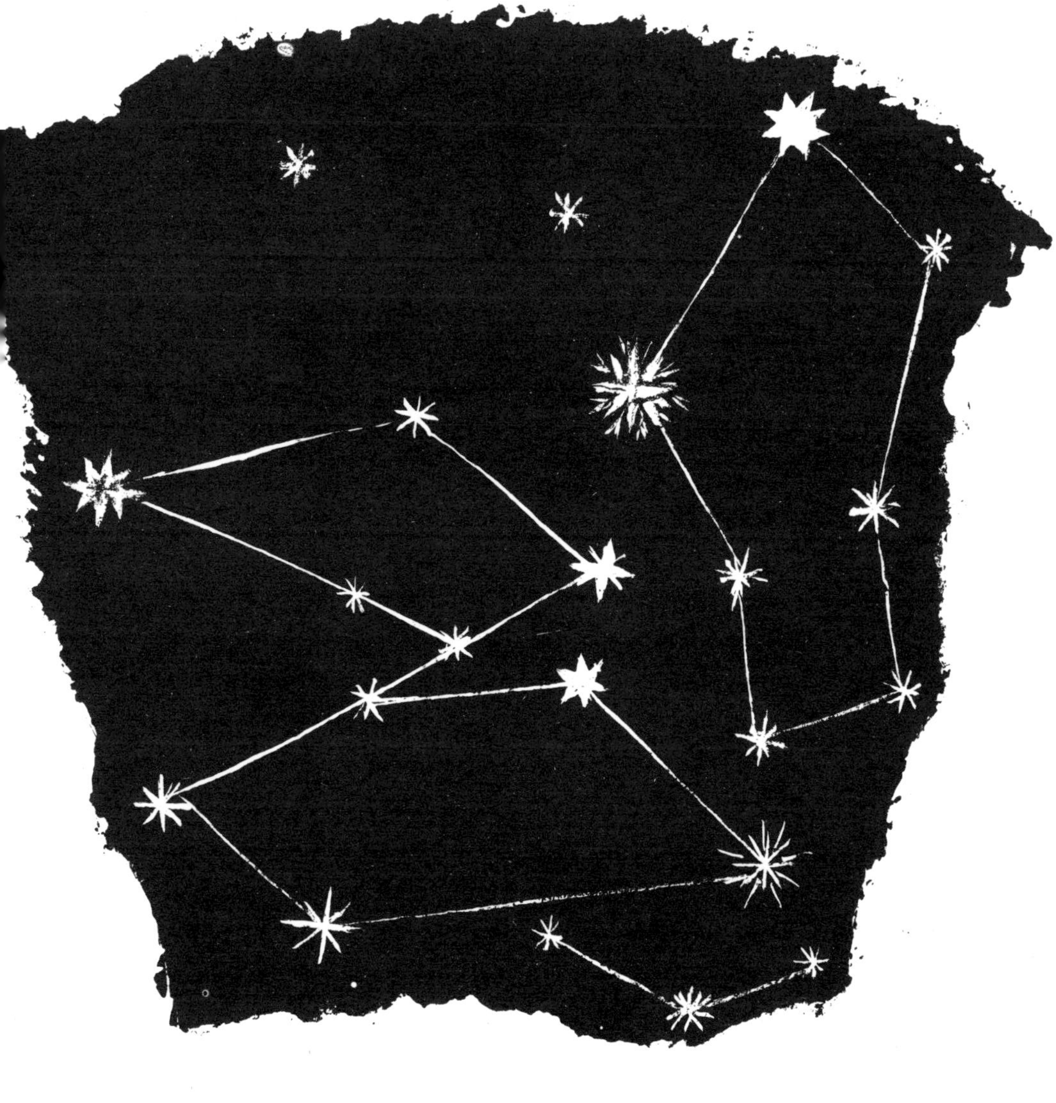

Pola
ILLYRIA
ADRIATIC SEA
TYRRHENIAN SEA
HELLAS
THESSALY
MOUNT PELION
Iolkos
Pagasae
Delphi
BOEOTIA
Thebes
Corinth
Athens
CYCLADES
AEGEAN SEA
Samothrace
LEMNOS
Myrine
TROY
CAPE MALLEA

The Voyage of the Argo

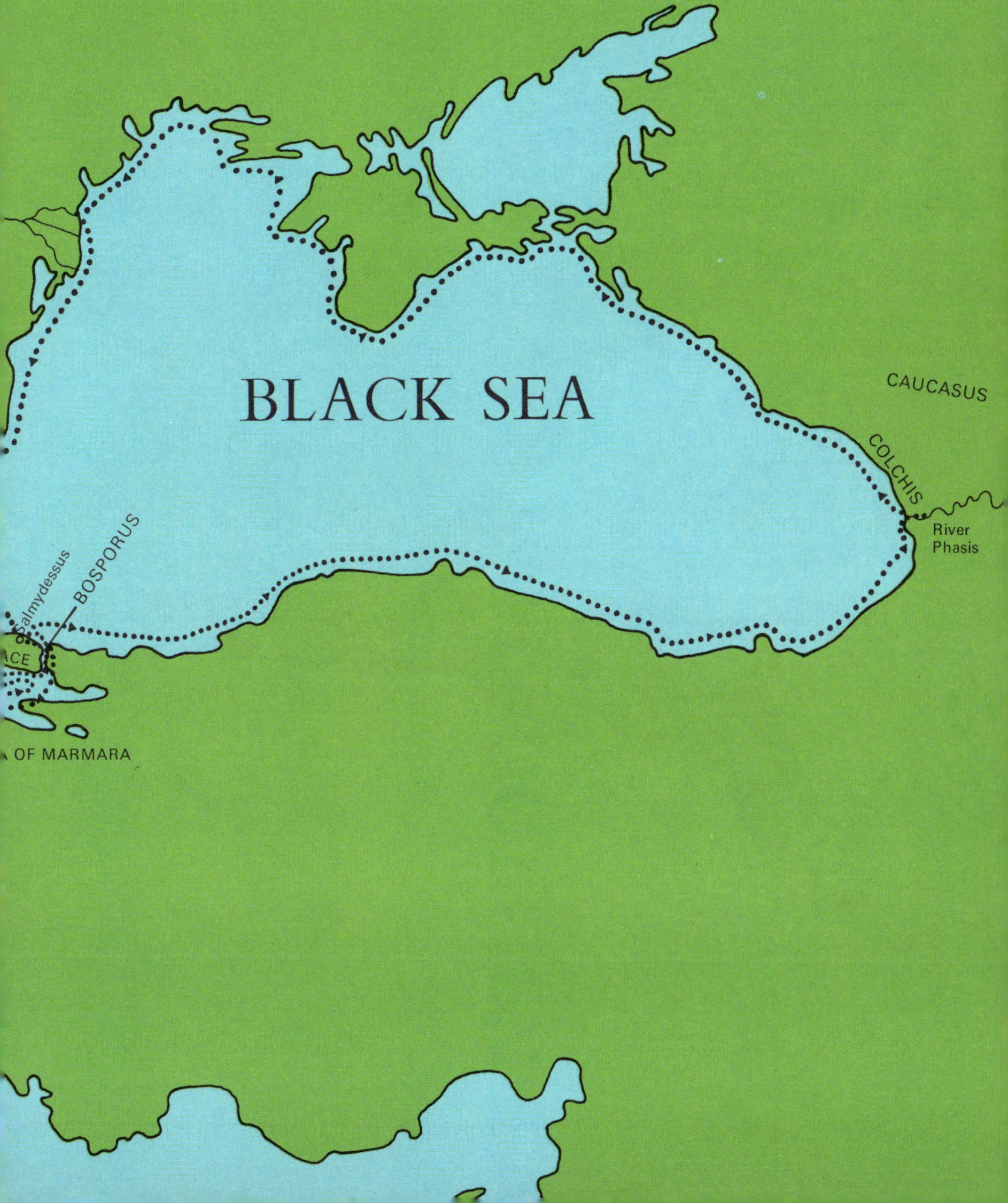

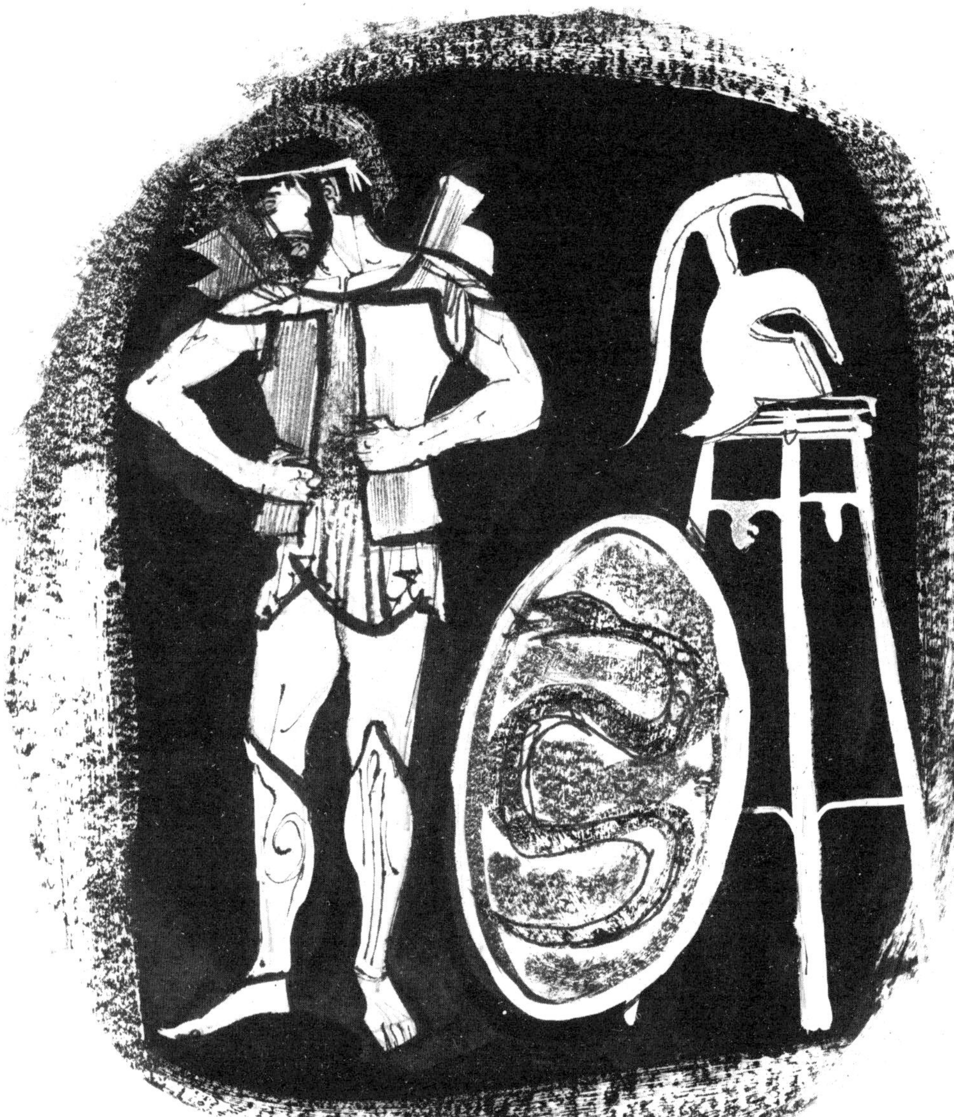

Achilles

The Story of
ACHILLES

GODS AND GODDESSES

IN THE STORY OF ACHILLES

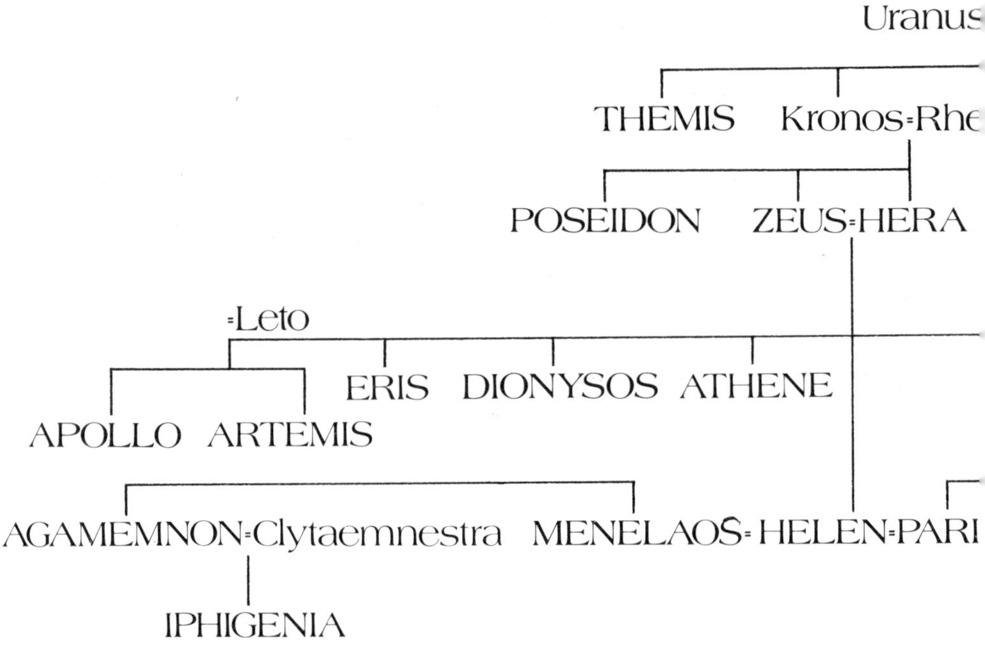

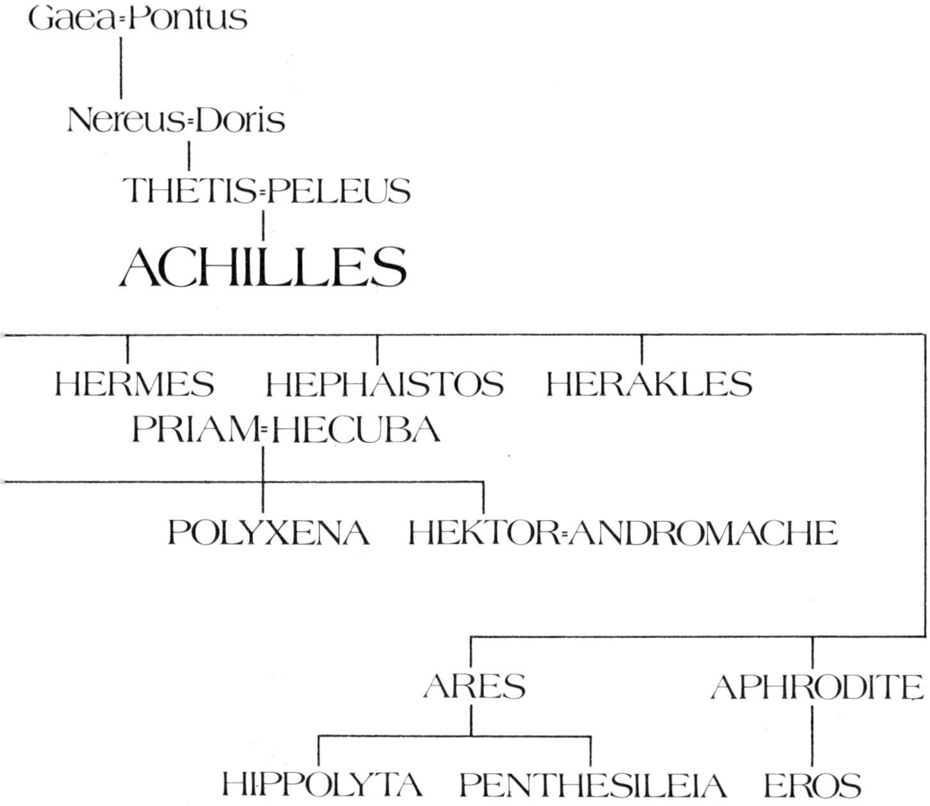

This family tree shows the gods and goddesses of ancient Greece, and the demigods and mortals related to them, whose lives are linked with that of Achilles, the hero of this story of once upon a time. Those whose names are in capitals—for example, ATHENE and PARIS—played a direct part in Achilles' adventures. Those whose names are not in capitals—such as Leto, mother of APOLLO—take their places in the tree as links in the line of descent from Gaea, the Earth-mother. It was believed in that world of long ago that Gaea was created out of Chaos. She brought forth Uranus (Heaven) and Pontus (Sea), by both of whom she then had children. From her were descended all the other gods and goddesses of Greece.

Achilles

Once upon a time there was a beautiful sea-nymph called Thetis, who was one of the Nereids, the daughters of a minor sea-god called Nereus. Zeus, the father of gods and men, and Poseidon, his brother and god of the sea, were rivals for her hand. But Thetis refused to marry either. Zeus she refused out of love and gratitude to his wife Hera, who had brought her up. Poseidon she refused because she felt that the other Nereids would be jealous if the great god of the sea set her above them as queen.

Both Zeus and Poseidon were disappointed by their failure to win Thetis. But their disappointment turned to relief when Themis, the goddess of law and order, told them the Fates had prophesied that any son of Thetis would grow up to be greater than his father. They agreed that they had had a lucky escape and decided that, to avoid trouble to the gods, Thetis must marry a mortal.

Their choice fell upon Peleus, a mighty hunter and warrior who was much loved by the gods. Peleus was one of the Heroes who had been brought up by the centaur Cheiron in his cave on Mount Pelion. One of Peleus's companions on Pelion had been Jason, and Peleus had been one of the first to answer Jason's appeal for volunteers to sail in the *Argo* to bring back the Golden Fleece to

A beautiful sea-nymph called Thetis

Hellas. Peleus happened to be visiting his old tutor on Mount Pelion when the decision was taken that he was to be the mortal husband of one of the immortal Nereids. Cheiron broke the news to him.

"But you will be wise, my son, to win Thetis's love. She has a strong mind of her own, and I do not think even the great Zeus himself could force her to marry you against her will."

"What shall I do to win her love?" Peleus asked.

"There is a tiny islet close to the shore at the foot of Pelion. On this islet is a small cave whose entrance is almost hidden by a bush of myrtle. It is Thetis's habit to rest in that cave after bathing. You must hide in the cave, and when she comes in you must take her in your arms. She will resist you and turn herself into all kinds of dangerous shapes to make you let go of her. But, if you can stand the pain you will suffer, she will yield at last."

So Peleus went down to the shore and swam out to the islet. Here he hid himself in the cave and waited. And then over the wine-dark sea came a bridled dolphin on whose back the lovely Nereid was riding. Peleus watched her bathing, fascinated by her grace and beauty. When at last she walked to the cave to rest, he sprang out from behind his hiding place and held her tightly. Thetis instantly turned herself into fire and burned him; then she turned into a cuttlefish and squirted ink all over him; then she became a lion that tore him with its claws; then she became a serpent and struck at him with her fangs.

In spite of being burned and blistered, blinded, mauled, and stung, Peleus did not loosen his hold. Finally Thetis surrendered, and they passionately embraced.

The wedding ceremony and feast was timed for the full moon, and the twelve gods of Olympus decided to attend the wedding. Hera was responsible for this decision. Nowhere in all the rich mythology of Greece is there any other instance of the gods attending a mortal wedding. Hera sent Iris, her rainbow-winged messenger, to invite all the older gods as well as the twelve Olympians. Unfortunately, one of the older immortals—Eris, the ugly goddess of strife—was overlooked. However, she attended the wedding uninvited and, just as the guests were about to drink to the bride and bridegroom, she rolled a golden apple into the assembly.

Peleus quickly picked it up. Then he saw that it carried an inscription. It read: *To the Fairest.*

Zeus saw that Hera, Aphrodite, and Athene were waiting expectantly for Peleus to present the golden apple to one of them.

"Give the apple to me," Zeus commanded.

And the embarrassed Peleus gratefully obeyed.

The golden apple would one day be known as the Apple of Discord, but at the time the interruption it caused was soon forgotten. The nine Muses began to sing an epithalamium, or wedding song. On the white beach below Mount Pelion, the Nereids danced as lightly as the wavelets themselves.

Thetis turned herself into fire

The Olympians' wedding gift to Peleus was a suit of golden armor. Poseidon gave him two of his immortal horses. Athene's gift was a spear whose blade had been forged by Hephaistos, god of fire and forger of metals.

After the marriage, Zeus ordered Peleus to capture Iolkos, the town in Thessaly from which the Argonauts had sailed. Zeus turned a swarm of ants, or Myrmidons, into an army, and with them Peleus afterward reigned in Iolkos as King of the Myrmidons.

In the course of time, the son who was to be greater than his sire was born to Thetis. He was named Achilles. Although he was born mortal, because he had a mortal father, Thetis longed for him to be immortal like herself. So she took the baby and dipped him into the Styx, the river of the Underworld. Achilles had now only one vulnerable spot—his right heel, by which his mother held him when she immersed him in the river.

At about this same time, in another country, there was born another baby boy, who was to play a decisive role in the future of Achilles. He was the son of King Priam and Queen Hecuba of Troy, that mighty city on the Asiatic side of the Hellespont. His name was Paris. A few days before he was born, his mother had dreamed that she had brought forth a firebrand from which issued innumerable flames in the shape of snakes. She had awakened from her nightmare screaming that the city of Troy and the forests of Mount Ida were burning. Priam, worried by the dream, consulted one of his seers who told him that the dream was a warning; the child Queen Hecuba was carrying would one day bring ruin to mighty Troy. King Priam then consulted a priest of Apollo, who confirmed the seer's interpretation and advised Priam to order the midwives to strangle the infant at birth. But, when Paris was born, Priam ordered Hecuba herself to kill him. Naturally, she refused. Then Priam ordered his herdsman Agelaos to kill the baby.

Agelaos could not bring himself to strangle or stab the infant. Instead, he took it to Mount Ida and left it there to die of exposure. Five days later he went back to assure himself that the baby was dead, so that he could tell his master that his orders had been carried out. But, to his amazement, he found the baby alive, being suckled by a she-bear. He could harden his heart no longer. He picked up the baby boy and carried him to his own home to be brought up with his own children.

Achilles, too, had an unusual infancy. When he was two years old, Thetis had a presentiment that he would lose his life in battle when he was only a young man. So, to save him from this fate, she proposed to have him brought up as a girl. Peleus, naturally, opposed this, and so Thetis left him and went back to live in her grotto under the sea. Peleus thereupon took his small son up to the cave on Mount Pelion to be brought up by the centaur Cheiron.

The young Achilles, fed by Cheiron on honey and the bone-marrow of fawns, learned to run faster than any of his age in all Hellas. He became so strong that, it is said, he

Achilles was dipped into the Styx

killed his first boar when he was six years old. Cheiron encouraged his athletic powers, but took care to train his mind as well as his body. The Muse Kalliope taught him music and song; Cheiron himself taught him medicine.

And now came tragedy. In the course of his Fourth Labor, the hunting of the Erymanthian boar, the mighty Herakles visited Mount Pelion and enjoyed Cheiron's hospitality. Young Achilles was proud to be presented to Herakles, who was already famous all over Hellas. But one day Cheiron was accidentally wounded in the knee by one of the deadly poisoned arrows of Herakles. In his agony he besought Almighty Zeus to take from him his immortality, so that death might end his suffering. Zeus granted the request and took Cheiron up into the heavens as the constellation Sagittarius.

After the death of Cheiron, Thetis reclaimed her son and took him to live with her on the island of Skyros. Here Achilles was brought up as a girl at the court of King Lykomedes, and here he stayed until he was about fifteen, when Peleus decided that he would no longer permit his only son to be brought up in this way.

"Zeus is planning a mighty war, with many woes for Hellas," argued Thetis. "I do not want my beloved son to be killed in battle while he is still young."

"But you made him invulnerable by dipping him into the Styx," Peleus retorted.

"Almost invulnerable," Thetis murmured sadly, remembering that unprotected heel.

However, Peleus was firm. He insisted that Achilles must have a male tutor. Unwillingly, Thetis agreed.

The tutor Peleus chose for Achilles was a distant kinsman called Phoinix, who had taken refuge with Peleus after his father had blinded him in a jealous rage. Peleus had taken Phoinix to Cheiron, who had restored his sight. Since then Phoinix had remained in Iolkos.

Achilles became very fond of his new tutor, and at the same time he started a devoted friendship with a youth a year or two older than himself whose name was Patrokles.

Away on Mount Ida the young Paris had kept pace with Achilles' athletic ability. He astonished the other herdsmen by his strength and skill and his handsome countenance and perfect figure.

Paris fell in love with a nymph called Oenone, who passionately returned his love. She used to accompany him on his hunting expeditions and applaud his handling of the herds. One of Paris's diversions was to set the bulls in Agelaos's herd against one another, crowning the victor with flowers and the loser with straw. Soon one of the bulls in the herd established his supremacy over all the others. Paris challenged the other herdsmen on Mount Ida to produce a bull that could defeat his champion. None could do so. Now Paris offered to pit his bull against any in Phrygia or Lydia, and promised to put a golden crown on the horns of the victor.

Ares, the god of war, told the other Olympians that for a joke he was going to turn himself into a bull and

The bull was crowned with flowers

fight Paris's champion. He invited them to watch the contest from Olympus. When Ares won, and Paris immediately and without argument crowned his horns with gold, the Olympians were all much impressed by the good manners of a simple herdsman.

"He is no simple herdsman," revealed Apollo. "He is a son of Priam. And my priest in Troy foretold that he would one day bring destruction to that city."

Thetis had been right when she had told Peleus that Zeus was planning a mighty war. Zeus had made up his mind that the populations both of Hellas and of the Asiatic side of the Hellespont must be reduced. To achieve this end, he intended to embroil Europe and Asia in war. Remembering the golden apple that Eris had rolled among the guests at Peleus's wedding, he decided to use it to stir up trouble. Hera, Athene, and Aphrodite had all expected to receive the apple from Peleus. Now Paris should decide who was the fairest of the three and award to her the golden apple. The three goddesses agreed to abide by the choice of the handsome young herdsman, and Paris, unwillingly, accepted the role of judge.

The goddesses argued for a while whether they should be judged clothed or unclothed. Athene was determined that Aphrodite should not wear her magic girdle, which made anybody she desired fall in love with her. Aphrodite for her part insisted that Athene should take off her helmet. So, in the end, it was agreed that all three should disrobe and appear naked in front of Paris.

Paris requested that each of the three goddesses should present herself before him in turn, out of sight and out of hearing of the others.

Hera, the Queen of Heaven, was the first. As Paris gazed in awe at her glorious figure, Hera told him that if he awarded her the golden apple she would make him the most powerful of all mortals and a ruler of many cities. Next came Athene, who promised him wisdom and victory in war. Lastly came Aphrodite, who promised him the most beautiful of mortal women—Helen.

"But she is the wife of King Menelaos of Sparta, the brother of the High King Agamemnon."

"I will take you to Sparta with my son Eros, and Helen will fall so passionately in love with you that she will follow you wherever you go."

Paris could not resist; he awarded the Apple of Discord to Aphrodite, and so made Hera and Athene his enemies.

How King Priam discovered that Paris was the son he believed was dead and how Paris went to Sparta and, with the help of Eros and Aphrodite, persuaded Helen to elope with him to Troy, must wait for another tale.

Menelaos appealed to his brother, King Agamemnon of Mycenae, for help. He wanted Agamemnon to lead an army against Troy to recover Helen and the treasure she had taken with her from Sparta.

The High King Agamemnon summoned all the kings and princes of Hellas to unite in assembling an army and a fleet to invade the Troad and bring back Helen to

Aphrodite, the fairest of them all

Menelaos. When Helen had chosen Menelaos to wed her, the many other suitors she had rejected had all sworn to stand behind Menelaos in future, and all of them declared their willingness to keep their vow. Kalchas, a renegade Trojan, much esteemed as an infallible prophet, now told Agamemnon that Troy could never be taken unless the young Achilles was with the invading fleet and army.

Agamemnon's chief adviser was Nestor, King of Pylos, the wisest of all the Greeks. He was now at least sixty years old but still able to fight. Nestor agreed to go to Iolkos and persuade Peleus to let his son join in the expedition. Nestor took with him Odysseus, the young King of Ithaka, whom he regarded as the heir to his wisdom. Nestor and Odysseus had no difficulty in persuading Peleus to let Achilles go. Peleus himself was now too old for active service.

Both Phoinix and Patrokles were delighted when Peleus agreed to let Achilles join the expedition with an army of Myrmidons and fifty ships. Peleus gave young Achilles the spear that had been Athene's wedding gift to him. He even gave him the two immortal horses that had been Poseidon's wedding present to him. One stipulation he did make: Achilles and his Myrmidons were not to be under the command of the High King Agamemnon.

At this time the Greek armies and ships were gathering at Aulis, where the island of Euboea is separated from the mainland of Hellas by no more than one hundred yards of sea. Helped by a northeast gale, Achilles reached Aulis safely with all his ships. But that same northeast gale prevented the Greek fleet from sailing against Troy.

Kalchas the seer told Agamemnon that the goddess Artemis was angry with him because he had killed one of her sacred hinds when out hunting. Kalchas went on to tell the High King that he could appease the anger of Artemis only by sacrificing his daughter Iphigeneia.

But Iphigeneia was in Mycenae. Agamemnon had to find an excuse for bringing her to Aulis. At the suggestion of Odysseus, he pretended that he wanted Iphigeneia to come to Aulis to marry the young Achilles.

When Achilles heard how his name had been used to deceive Iphigeneia, he was furious with Agamemnon. It was the beginning of a bitter hostility between Agamemnon and Achilles.

Achilles tried his utmost to save Iphigeneia from being sacrificed. He threatened to withdraw his Myrmidons and his ships from the expedition. He even declared his willingness to marry her. But Iphigeneia shook her head.

"No, no, I must die for the glory of Hellas."

And with these words she laid her head upon the block and awaited the sacrificial ax.

Suddenly there came a peal of thunder. The northeast gale instantly died away. The goddess Artemis came down, seized Iphigeneia and carried her off to become one of her priestesses at her temple in Tauris.

Just before the fleet sailed, Agamemnon was sacrificing to Zeus when a large serpent with blood-red spots over it

Peleus gave the two immortal horses

wriggled out from the altar and up into a plane tree, where a small bird had a nest and eight young ones. The serpent devoured all of them, then, as the mother-bird fluttered around, caught her in its jaws also. Then it coiled itself around the trunk of the tree. There was a flash of lightning and Zeus turned the serpent to stone. The seer Kalchas, called upon to interpret this strange incident, declared it meant that the war with Troy would last for nine years and that in the tenth year Troy would fall at last.

When the fleet sailed there was another violent storm. In the confusion the pilots lost their direction. Instead of landing in the Troad, they beached the ships in Mysia, which is the country south of Phrygia. The Mysians, finding themselves invaded by a strange army, fought back with determination and courage. Led by their King, Telephos, they drove the Greeks back to their ships. But Achilles and Patrokles quickly rallied the Greeks and put Telephos and his men to flight.

The Greeks had duly sacrificed to Dionysos before sailing, but the Mysians had for some time been neglecting the god of wine. To punish Telephos, Dionysos made a vine spring up in front of him as he ran. Telephos tripped, and was wounded in the thigh from a thrust by the invincible spear that Peleus had given to Achilles. The Greeks, anxious only to reach Troy, then left Mysia.

King Telephos's wound refused to heal and he went to consult the Oracle at Delphi. He was answered in the usual ambiguous style of the Oracle: "He that woundeth thee shall also heal thee." Telephos disguised himself as a beggar and went to Mycenae, where Agamemnon, after the muddle made of the first attempt to reach Troy, was busy reorganizing the Greek forces. Agamemnon had no desire to antagonize the Mysians, lest they decided to ally themselves to the Trojans. He asked Achilles to heal Telephos as the Oracle had foretold.

Achilles protested that any medicine he had ever been taught by Cheiron had long been forgotten. Odysseus, clever as usual, suggested that, as it was the spear that had wounded Telephos, some scrapings from it might heal the wound. This was a success, and Telephos went back to Mysia on good terms with the Greeks.

The Greek fleet now reached the small island of Tenedos, which is close to the Troad on the mainland. Here, under Agamemnon's orders, they waited for the return of Odysseus and Menelaos, who had gone to Troy with an ultimatum demanding the return of Helen and of the treasure she had taken from Sparta when she eloped with Paris. The ultimatum was refused.

Tenedos was ruled by a son of Apollo called Tenes. Before he had set out to join the expedition against Troy, Achilles had been warned by his mother that he must never kill a son of Apollo—because if he did Apollo would for ever afterward be his enemy and would ultimately ensure his death.

Tenes was furious when the Greek fleet came to Tenedos, and in order to show his enmity he went to the

A strange serpent appeared

top of a high cliff and hurled a great rock down on the Greek fleet. It fell close to one of the ships of the Myrmidons. In a rage Achilles jumped overboard and swam ashore. As soon as he came face to face with Tenes he thrust that deadly spear of his through Tenes's heart. Then he suddenly realized what he had done. He buried Tenes where he lay and was angered with Agamemnon for allowing the Greeks to land and ravage Tenedos.

The Greeks now sailed from Tenedos and beached their ships within sight of Troy. Achilles was on the point of leaping ashore when he remembered another of his mother's warnings. She had told him that the first Greek ashore in the Troad would inevitably be killed. So Achilles held back, and it was Protesilaos, a Thessalian prince, who was killed. For a time the Trojans managed to keep the Greeks from disembarking in force, but when Achilles landed he and his Myrmidons drove the Trojans back and the Greeks were able to land.

At that date siege warfare was completely undeveloped and the Greeks never supposed they would be able to conquer Troy by direct attack. All they could hope to do was to wear down Troy by isolating it and destroying its trade. The tale of the city's nine years of siege tends to be a monotonous list of battles in which the Olympians often played a part, Aphrodite and Apollo helping the Trojans, Hera, Athene, and Poseidon the Greeks.

By the beginning of the tenth year of the war, Troy was still impregnable, but the Trojans were feeling the strain on their resources through loss of trade. It was on one of the many expeditions to ravage the country around Troy, in the spring of the tenth year, when the great Trojan irises were in flower beside the river Scamander, that Chryseis, the daughter of Chryses, one of Apollo's priests, was awarded to Agamemnon as his share of the spoils. At the same time a beautiful girl called Briseis was allotted to Achilles.

Chryses was much upset by the capture of his beautiful daughter and offered Agamemnon a ransom for her return. Agamemnon had been much attracted by Chryseis and refused. So the priest prayed to Apollo to punish the Greeks. Apollo, who of all the Olympians was by now the bitterest enemy of the Greeks, at once answered his priest's appeal by sending a plague of dysentery into the Greek camp. Kalchas told Nestor and Odysseus why the plague had been sent and urged them to restore Chryseis to her father. For some time Agamemnon refused, but as the plague increased he unwillingly gave way. When Chryseis was given back to her father the plague immediately ceased.

Although Agamemnon was praised for his unselfish action, he still begrudged it and he was resentful that Achilles had been able to keep Briseis without any interference, human or divine. He had always been jealous of Achilles' renown as a warrior. So, now he seized Briseis.

Achilles, who was in love with Briseis, was furious with Agamemnon for this high-handed action.

Tenes challenged the Greek fleet

"I have had enough of that swollen-headed Achaean," he told Patrokles. "My Myrmidons and I are not Achaeans. Let them get on with the war as best they can without me. We fight no more to help them against Troy, and as soon as possible we shall return to Thessaly."

Patrokles was depressed to hear this. He was thoroughly enjoying himself in the war. However, when Achilles withdrew to his tent and ordered his Myrmidons to take no part in the fighting even if the Trojans tried to overrun the Greek camp, Patrokles remained silent. He knew how idle it would be to argue with Achilles in his present mood.

Without Achilles, the Greeks were soon hard beset by the Trojans. Ajax and Diomedes and Odysseus fought valiantly, but, under the leadership of Hektor, the noblest and most valiant of Priam's sons, the Trojans drove the Greeks back into their camp.

Realizing the danger, the leading Greek warriors implored Nestor to persuade Agamemnon to lay aside his pride and return Briseis to Achilles.

Nestor managed to convince Agamemnon that the war would end disastrously for the Greeks unless Achilles could be induced to fight again.

It must be admitted that when Agamemnon decided to apologize to Achilles he apologized handsomely. An embassy consisting of Odysseus and Phoinix, the old tutor of Achilles, whom he loved and respected, offered on behalf of Agamemnon to restore Briseis and pay a large sum of gold. If the war against Troy should end in victory for the Greeks, Agamemnon offered Achilles any one of his three daughters in marriage, and seven cities as her dowry.

Odysseus raised every argument he could think of to persuade Achilles to accept this magnificent offer, but Achilles sat in silent gloom. Then old Phoinix did his utmost by talking about the days when Peleus took his son away from Skyros to dress him as a boy again.

"Would your old tutor give you bad advice, my son? Remember that it was I who persuaded your noble father to let you leave for Aulis with fifty ships. Remember that it was I who persuaded him to give you his suit of golden armor, his wedding present from the Olympians, and the deadly spear given him by the goddess Athene, and even the two immortal horses given by Poseidon. Listen to me, do listen to me, my son, and harness those horses to your chariot and wield again that deadly spear."

But Achilles sat obstinately silent.

The continued absence of Achilles from the battlefield around Troy made the Trojans bolder and bolder. At last, they made a full-scale assault on the Greek camp.

The Greeks had taken advantage of an armistice to build a wall behind the trench that defended their encampment. To their consternation the wall was breached, and to their still greater dismay a torch flung by Hektor set fire to the first ship the Greeks had beached ten years ago, the ship of Protesilaos.

Even Achilles was shaken for a moment.

The ship of Protesilaos was set on fire

"No matter," he said to Patrokles. "Provided our own ships are not fired we shall be sailing back to Thessaly in a day or two."

However, Patrokles continued to argue with him.

"Suppose they do succeed in firing our ships, how shall we ever reach Thessaly? I beg you to let me lead your Myrmidons into the fight. Let me wear your golden armor and the Trojans, thinking it is you fighting them, will draw back."

Achilles still hesitated.

"I beg you to listen to me," Patrokles urged. "I beg you to let me drive the Trojans back from our encampment, and save the ships from being burned."

Achilles could not help being moved by what was almost agony in the voice of his dearest friend.

"So be it," he said at last.

So Patrokles put on the golden armor. But when he armed himself with his friend's deadly spear, Achilles said, in a voice that Patrokles knew he must not argue with, "No, no, the armor is enough. You might lose my spear in battle. Moreover, Athene might be offended if I lent the spear she gave my father to anyone else. With Apollo so active on behalf of the Trojans we need all the help that Athene and great Hera can give us."

So Patrokles, wearing the golden armor and rallying the Myrmidons, attacked the Trojans. They supposed that he was the invincible Achilles himself, and retreated in confusion. In the exhilaration of his success, Patrokles reached the very walls of Troy. He even wondered whether it was to fall to him to lead the Greeks in a final victorious assault upon the city that had withstood ten long years of siege. Then, suddenly, he found himself facing a gleaming shield. Behind the shield was Apollo himself. Always active on behalf of the Trojans, the god feared that Patrokles might indeed inspire the Greeks to scale the walls of Troy in sufficient numbers to overcome the garrison. It is possible that Apollo mistook Patrokles for Achilles. At any rate, he cast a mist over him and buffeted him so severely that Patrokles was so dazed he hardly knew if he was still standing on his feet. At that moment the great Hektor, who had been fighting hard to rally the Trojans, encountered Patrokles and, after a short duel, killed him and stripped the armor from his corpse.

There was now a desperate struggle for the body of Patrokles, which many of the Trojans still thought to be the body of Achilles.

When the news of Patrokles' death was brought to Achilles, he rushed unarmed from his tent in a frenzy of grief. The sound of his war cry ringing out after so long a silence had such an effect on the Trojans that the Greeks were able to recover Patrokles' body.

When he saw the corpse of his beloved friend, Achilles threw himself down beside it, and in paroxysms of grief mourned for his lost companion of so many years.

"And it was I who killed him," he sobbed. "Why did I consent to lend him my armor? Why did I mind whether

Patrokles goes into battle

the Trojans fired our ships or not? O Patrokles, my beloved Patrokles, where are you now?"

Suddenly he leaped up and, without armor, rushed toward the battle. Odysseus managed to restrain him and persuaded him to hold back until Hephaistos could forge for him a new suit of armor.

Achilles agreed to wait for the armor, which was to be brought to him next day, but he was determined to meet and kill Hektor before the funeral of Patrokles.

When, on the following day, Achilles appeared duly armed, such was the fury of his attack that the Trojans broke into three groups, the larger body quickly retreating across the plain toward the city walls. Achilles drove the rest of the Trojan forces into a bend of the river Scamander. Here they would all have perished if Achilles had not been so intent on coming face to face with Hektor. The noblest of the sons of Priam had been badly bruised by a large stone flung at him by Ajax during the fight for the body of Patrokles. However, he felt that, at whatever cost to himself, he could not seem to be afraid to answer the challenge of Achilles to single combat. So, though feeling far from fit to meet the most formidable of all the Greeks, Hektor decided he must accept the challenge. When he came out from the city gates, Greeks and Trojans drew back to watch this mortal combat between the two greatest warriors of the small world of long ago.

Hektor, realizing how seriously that blow from a stone had handicapped him, thought of a way in which he in his turn could handicap his opponent. For weeks now, Achilles had been sitting in his tent without taking any exercise, let alone fighting. He was probably already rather short of breath. If he could be made still more breathless, then Hektor might be able to hold out against him until sundown. Then the combat would have to be resumed next day, by which time Hektor might have recovered his strength.

So, to the amazement of all those who had lowered their arms to watch, Hektor began to run away around the city walls. Twice around the city walls Achilles pursued him; but, alas for Hektor's hopes, when he turned and stood to face Achilles the latter was not in the least breathless. He did not wait to draw his sword but drove his deadly spear into Hektor's breast.

As the noblest of Priam's sons lay dying, he gasped an appeal to Achilles to allow his body to be ransomed for burial. Achilles grimly shook his head.

"You killed my dearest friend," he said, "and for that your body shall rot unburied."

From brutal speech Achilles went on to much more brutal action. He stripped the armor from the dead body of the once mighty Hektor, and sent it back to the Greek encampment. Then he slit through the flesh behind the tendons of Hektor's heels and with leather thongs fastened them to his chariot. When the body was firmly secured, Achilles got into his chariot and, whipping up its three white horses, drove three times around the walls of Troy.

Hektor's body dragged around the walls

It was an agonizing sight for Hektor's devoted wife Andromache to see that body she had loved so deeply being dragged along in a cloud of dust. When Achilles had exulted sufficiently in the piteous sight he was offering to the people of Troy, he drove slowly back to the Greek encampment. There he left the body of Hektor lying unattended under the hot sun while he began the preparations for the funeral of Patrokles.

Warriors were sent off to gather timber, and the largest funeral pyre ever raised was built to cremate the corpse of Patrokles. Cattle were sacrificed, and two of the hounds from the pack of nine with which Patrokles had hunted. Achilles, still indulging in what was beginning to seem unreasonable grief for his dead friend, was on the point of throwing the body of Hektor to the seven remaining hounds when Aphrodite restrained him.

"You have already incurred my ill will by attacking my son Aeneas and driving away his flocks from Mount Ida. Beware, Achilles, of my enmity."

Achilles refrained from throwing the corpse of Hektor to the pack, but after the funeral games were over he continued to indulge his grief by rising every day at dawn to lash the corpse of Hektor to his chariot and drag it three times around the funeral pyre of Patrokles. Apollo, now more than ever an enemy of Achilles, preserved the body from being corrupted.

Thetis now appealed to Father Zeus himself to make it possible for her to offer the body of Hektor for ransom.

She was dreading the hostility of Apollo and Aphrodite and hoped to prevent Achilles from giving them any further offence. Zeus listened to her plea and sent Hermes to escort King Priam one night to where Achilles lay fast asleep in his tent. Hermes woke Achilles and advised him to grant Priam's request to ransom the body of his son so that it might be given burial. He added that Achilles should realize that Priam might easily have strangled him while he was sleeping so heavily. The messenger of the Olympians vanished, leaving Priam and Achilles to talk alone. Achilles agreed to Priam's request to ransom Hektor's body.

"What ransom do you demand?" Priam asked.

"A weight of gold equal to the body of your son," Achilles replied.

Priam accepted the terms, although he knew that his treasury, already depleted by the heavy financial strain of the war, would be almost emptied by this untoward further strain.

Achilles set up a huge pair of scales under the city walls. In one scale-pan the body of Hektor was placed; into the other were placed ingots of gold. From the city walls the Trojans looked down in anguish, because in spite of all the gold the weight of Hektor's body still kept the scale-pan with the gold aloft.

At last, when only a few inches were needed to raise the body to the same weight as the gold, Polyxena, the most beautiful of Priam's daughters, threw down from the

Hektor's body outweighed the gold

wall all her own bracelets and necklaces. They turned the scale, and a great shout of relief went up from the anxious spectators on the city walls; the body of the noblest Trojan would now be buried, with much public lamentation, among his own people.

Achilles was filled with admiration as he watched the Princess Polyxena giving away her own golden bracelets and necklaces to secure the body of her beloved brother. He saw Andromache embracing Polyxena with tears of gratitude, and in that moment fell passionately in love with the Trojan Princess. He told Priam that if he would give Polyxena to him in wedlock she should be the ransom for Hektor. Moreover, if Priam would persuade Paris to give Helen back to Menelaos he would use all his influence and do everything in his power to promote a lasting peace between Hellas and Troy.

Priam replied that for the present he was content to ransom Hektor's body with gold, but he added that if Achilles could persuade the Greeks to depart without Helen he would certainly be willing to grant him Polyxena's hand in marriage.

Achilles agreed to do what he could.

"Polyxena is the only woman I have desired in wedlock," he declared.

Priam then took the body of Hektor for burial.

Notwithstanding the strain upon the Trojan resources, the diminishing treasury, and the loss of trade, King Priam still had faithful allies. Some years before,

Penthesileia, the Queen of the Amazons, had accidentally killed her sister Hippolyta with an ill-aimed arrow while they were hunting. This had been a great anguish to Penthesileia and she had come to the court of King Priam for him to absolve her of the death of her beloved sister.

Now, to repay Priam for his kindness, she brought her Amazons from their country on the northern shore of the Pontus Euxinus, which we call the Black Sea.

Queen Penthesileia and her Amazons fought with such skill and courage that they did serious damage to the Greek forces. Penthesileia was a daughter of Ares, the god of war, and as formidable as she was beautiful. On two or three occasions, she compelled Achilles himself to retreat, but in the end he killed her. As she lay dying, Achilles, overwhelmed with remorse, took her in his arms and kissed her lips. Then he buried Penthesileia with his own hands and mourned for her.

Thetis knew that her son's death was now near at hand and in an attempt to propitiate Apollo she advised Achilles to go to Lesbos, where he offered sacrifices to Apollo, Artemis, and their mother Leto.

Back in the Troad, the Trojans, with the help of Memnon, the black King of Ethiopia, who had come from the farthest south of that small world of long ago, nearly succeeded in burning the Greek ships. They were driven back when Achilles returned and killed Memnon.

It was to be the last achievement of Achilles. While the battle raged by one of the gates of the impregnable city,

Ajax carried Achilles from the battlefielc

Apollo bade Paris shoot a poisoned arrow at Achilles and he directed that arrow to pierce Achilles in his right heel, his only vulnerable spot. It was poetic justice that Achilles, who had dragged Hektor by the heels three times around the city, should now die from a poisoned heel. There was a terrific fight for the corpse of Achilles but at last Ajax threw it over his shoulders and through a shower of arrows brought it back to the Greek camp.

Here for seventeen days Thetis and the Nereids mourned for Achilles, while the nine Muses chanted dirges. Thetis then went to Olympus to plead with Zeus to bestow immortality upon her son. Zeus, never able to resist a plea from Thetis, granted her request. While the funeral games were still in progress, Thetis descended from Olympus and took from the blazing fire the soul of Achilles. The home she chose for that soul was a little wooded island called Louke, which was close to the mouth of the Danube. Here for many years to come Achilles would be revered as a demi-god.

There is no space to tell here of the fall of Troy and of the wooden horse within which the Greeks passed through the gates of the city. But a word must be said about the end of Paris. He, too, was struck by a poisoned arrow. In his agony he managed to reach Mount Ida, where his happy youth had been spent, and to find Oenone, whom he had deserted to go in search of Helen. Oenone refused to give him herbs to soothe his pain, but when he died she was so unhappy that she killed herself.

The Travels of Achilles

BLACK SEA
Hellespont
TROAD
PHRYGIA
Troy
DOS
River Scamander
MOUNT IDA
MYSIA
ESBOS
LYDIA

Theseus

The Story of THESEUS

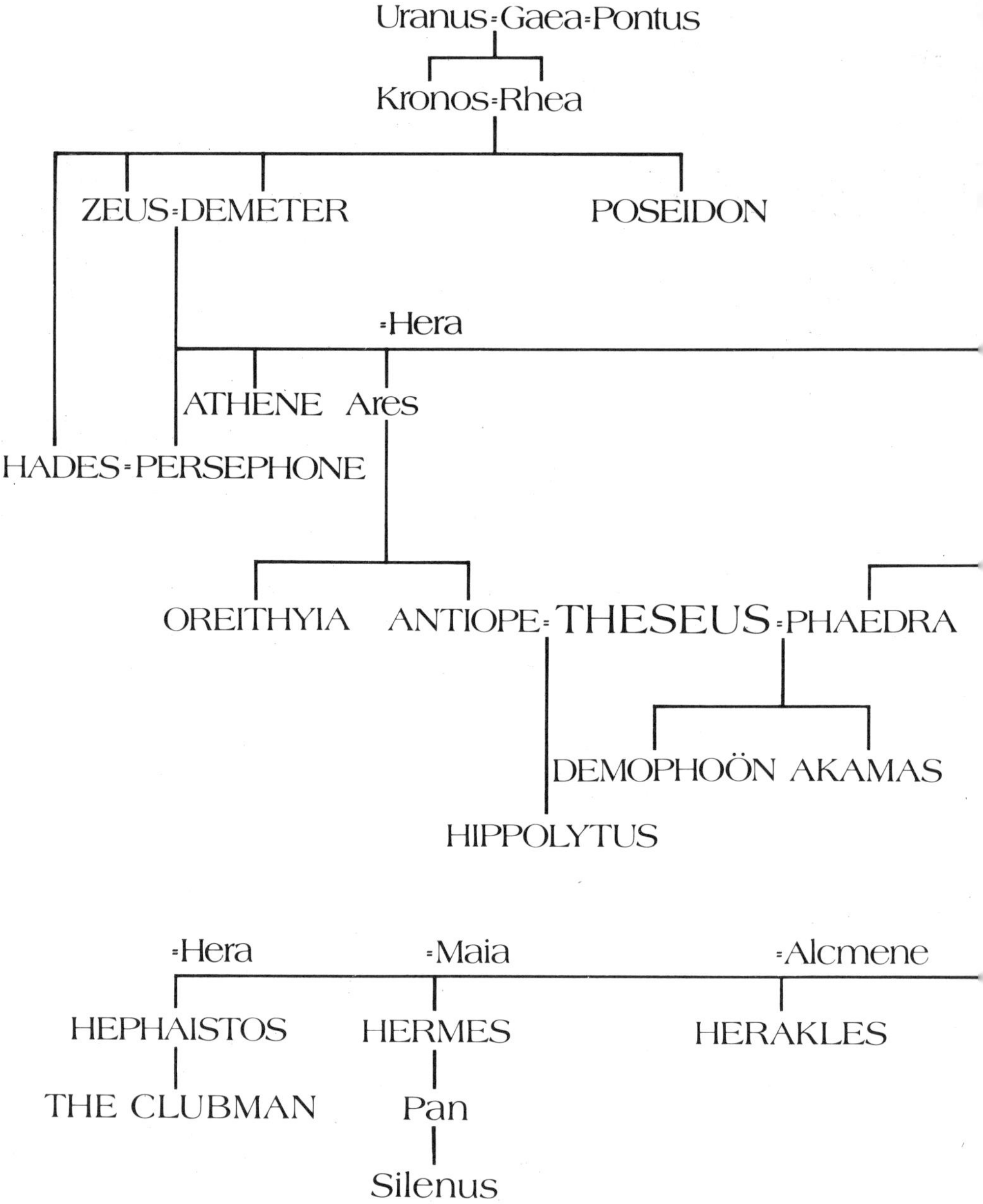
Uranus=Gaea=Pontus
Kronos=Rhea
ZEUS=DEMETER
POSEIDON
=Hera
ATHENE
Ares
HADES=PERSEPHONE
OREITHYIA
ANTIOPE=THESEUS=PHAEDRA
DEMOPHOÖN
AKAMAS
HIPPOLYTUS
=Hera
=Maia
=Alcmene
HEPHAISTOS
HERMES
HERAKLES
THE CLUBMAN
Pan
Silenus

GODS AND GODDESSES

IN THE STORY OF THESEUS

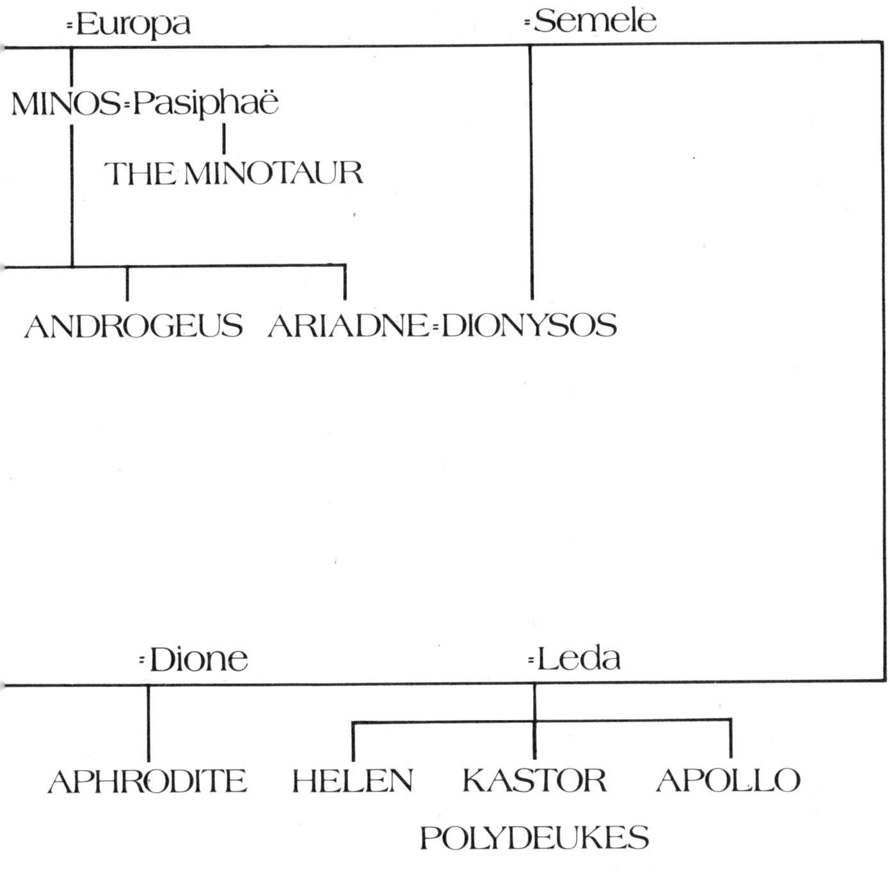

This family tree shows the gods and goddesses of ancient Greece, and the demi-gods and mortals related to them, whose lives are linked with that of Theseus, the hero of this story of once upon a time. Those whose names are in capitals—for example, MINOS and PHAEDRA—played a direct part in Theseus s adventures. Those whose names are not in capitals—such as Europa, mother of MINOS—take their places in the tree as links in the line of descent from Gaea, the Earth-mother. It was believed in that world of long ago that Gaea was created out of Chaos. She brought forth Uranus (Heaven) and Pontus (Sea), by both of whom she then had children. From her were descended all the other gods and goddesses of Greece.

Aegeus consulted the Delphic Oracle

Theseus

Once upon a time there was a King of Athens called Aegeus. His father had ruled over the whole of Attica, the part of Greece of which Athens was the capital, but when he died he left his kingdom to be divided between his four sons. To Aegeus, his best-loved son, he left Athens itself. His three other sons had to accept less important areas of Attica, and one of them, whose name was Pallas, was particularly jealous of Aegeus.

Aegeus had been twice married, but he had no son. This was a great disappointment to him, particularly since his brother and rival Pallas had many sons, all of whom seemed to be growing up into giants. So Aegeus went to consult the Oracle at Delphi to see what the future held for him. On his way back he stayed with his friend Pittheus, King of Troezen. Pittheus had a daughter called Aethra, and he suggested that Aegeus should marry her. Aegeus agreed, but he insisted that the marriage should remain a secret. He hoped that if his brother Pallas supposed him to be still without the prospect of a son he would stop his own huge sons from plotting to seize the throne of Athens.

So Aegeus married Aethra. But soon he had to leave her and return to Athens. Before he left Troezen, he buried his sword and sandals beneath a heavy rock, and told Aethra that, if she bore a son, she was to take him to the rock when he became sixteen years old. Then, if he was strong enough to move the rock aside, he was to buckle on the sword and wear the sandals and go to Athens to be recognized by Aegeus as his heir.

Some months after Aegeus left Troezen the son he longed for was born. The baby was named Theseus. His father's name was kept secret, because Pittheus and Aethra were afraid that, if it were known, the baby might be kidnapped or killed by rivals for the throne of Athens. They let it be whispered about that the baby's father was Poseidon, the mighty ruler of the sea. The news that he had a son and heir in Troezen was kept even from Aegeus.

Only one tale has come down to us about the childhood of Theseus, which was spent in the palace of his grandfather and guardian, Pittheus, at Troezen. Herakles, the strongest man on earth, paid a visit to Pittheus. One day, because it was very hot, Herakles took off the lion skin he wore as a souvenir of a lion he had killed with his own hands, and left it flung over a chair while he went into another room to talk with his host. Some of the children in the palace came in, saw the skin, and rushed away screaming in terror, thinking it was a living lion. Theseus, then aged seven, also mistook the skin for a real lion, but he neither screamed nor ran away. Instead, he calmly fetched an ax from beside a pile of logs and came back to attack the lion. So, even though he was only seven years old, Theseus already displayed that great courage for which one day he would be famous.

Nine more years passed, and it became time for Theseus to go to Delphi, there to offer his first haircut of manhood to Apollo in order to receive the god's goodwill. But Theseus did not like the idea of having the whole of his head shaved. He insisted on having only the front of it shaved, so that any adversary with whom he was in mortal combat would not be able to seize him by the forelock. He knew that no enemy would be able to grasp him by his back hair, because he would never turn his back on an opponent. That kind of haircut and shave became the fashion among young Hellenes and was called the Theseian tonsure.

When Theseus came back from Delphi his mother decided that the time had come for him to know who his father was. She took him to the rock under which Aegeus had hidden his sword and sandals and waited anxiously to see if her son would be strong enough to move the rock. She need not have worried. Theseus moved it easily and forthwith picked up his father's sword and put his feet into his father's sandals.

It was now time for Theseus to find his way to Athens and make himself known to King Aegeus. His grandfather and his mother both tried to persuade him to go by water across the Saronic Gulf, but Theseus obstinately refused to make the easy journey by boat. He was determined to walk around the gulf and across the narrow isthmus to

Theseus rolled aside the great stone

Attica. The more his grandfather and mother warned him of the dangers of the long journey by road, the more eager he was to go. The more dangers he encountered the more pleased he would be, for he was determined to emulate the famous deeds of the mighty Herakles.

So Theseus set out along that dangerous road from Troezen to Athens. He had made up his mind that he would not pick a quarrel with anybody he met on the way, but that if anybody deliberately quarreled with him he would pay him back in his own coin.

His determination was soon put to the test. At Epidaurus he was waylaid by the notorious Clubman, who was believed to be a son of Hephaistos, god of fire and forger of metals. The Clubman had earned his nickname from a huge brazen club he carried, a present from his father. Like Hephaistos himself, the Clubman walked with a limp, but he was brutally strong—strong enough to kill and rob every wayfarer unlucky enough to cross his path. He sprang out as Theseus passed, swinging his club to deal a death blow. But Theseus was too quick and too powerful. He wrested the brazen club from his savage assailant and with one powerful blow put an end to the Clubman's career as a threat to wayfarers. Theseus was delighted with his victory and felt the mighty Herakles would have much approved of it. From then on, he always armed himself with the brazen club.

Theseus tramped on until he reached the narrowest part of the isthmus that divides the Corinthian Gulf from the Saronic Gulf. But there he found the road barred by Sinis, nicknamed the Pine-bender. The grim joke that Sinis was in the habit of playing was to bend a pine tree over until its top touched the ground. Then he would ask a passer-by to help him hold the pine down. As soon as the stranger had put his arms around the trunk, Sinis would let go his hold; the pine would spring upright and catapult the wayfarer to his death.

But this was not his most cruel trick. Sometimes he would bend two pine trees down toward each other and tie a captive between them, an arm bound to each tree. Then he would let the trees spring apart and the victim would be torn asunder.

Theseus had been told of Sinis's cruelty and he resolved to punish him. They wrestled for a time, and gradually Theseus wore down the Pine-bender's great strength.

"You shall die by the death you have inflicted on others," Theseus said grimly.

With these words, he bent a pine tree over and sent Sinis hurtling to his death.

Theseus went on across the narrow isthmus until he came to a cliff-top high above the sea. There he saw a man sitting on a rock by the edge of the cliff. Theseus knew that this was Skiron, whose custom was to force passing wayfarers, under threat of death, to kneel down and wash his feet. When his victim knelt to perform this disagreeable task, Skiron would kick him over the cliff to be eaten by a huge turtle that swam in the sea below.

Theseus catapulted the Pine-bender to his death

But Theseus did not wait for Skiron to order him to kneel. He sprang forward and, before Skiron had time to rise from the rock on which he was sitting, Theseus picked him up and hurled him over the cliff.

After disposing of Skiron, Theseus walked on until he had left the isthmus behind him and was drawing near Eleusis in Attica. Pilgrims to the religious festival at this place, which was sacred to the goddess Demeter, had been terrorized by Kerkyon, a wrestler of great strength. Kerkyon would challenge the pilgrims to wrestle with him, and then crush the life from them with his powerful embrace. When Theseus arrived, Kerkyon challenged him to a bout, confident that this handsome young man would be an easy prey. How wrong he was! Theseus had been taught the art of wrestling, which is a matter not of brute strength, but of skill. He accepted Kerkyon's challenge, caught him under the knees, dashed him head first to the ground, and cracked his skull. For this deed Theseus earned the gratitude of Demeter.

Drawing near to Athens, Theseus came to a house whose hospitality he had been warned not to accept. This house belonged to Procrustes. In it were two beds, one short and the other long. Procrustes would offer some passer-by a night's lodging. If the lodger was a short man, Procrustes would put him in the long bed and then stretch his legs until his toes touched the end of it. A tall lodger he would put in the short bed and cut off the part of the wretched man's legs that protruded from the bed.

Theseus accepted Procrustes' offer of a night's lodging and turned the tables upon his host. Either he put Procrustes in the long bed and racked him to reach the end of it, or he put him in the short bed and cut off the end of his legs. Whichever he did, no more was heard of Procrustes and his cruelty.

Before going on to Athens to make himself known to his father Aegeus, Theseus was entertained by some friends of his who had been to Troezen and knew him as the grandson of Pittheus but did not know that he was the son of Aegeus. When they heard that Theseus intended to visit King Aegeus they gave him a long robe to wear.

When Theseus reached Athens he found that a new temple of Apollo was being built in the city. He strolled over to watch the work. A group of masons working on the roof, seeing his long robe and carefully plaited hair, mistook him for a girl, and began to shout after him.

"What are you doing walking about without anybody to look after you? A big girl like you ought to know better."

Theseus did not reply. He had already noticed the masons' ox-drawn cart standing in the street. He walked unhurriedly to it, unyoked the oxen, and tossed one of them into the air—about as high as the roof of the temple. Not surprisingly, the masons stopped taunting him.

While Theseus had been growing up in Troezen, his father, unaware of his existence, had given refuge to the sorceress Medea after she had fled from Corinth. Medea

The evil Skiron became food for the turtle

now hoped that by her magic spells she could persuade Aegeus to make her son Medos his heir.

When Theseus arrived in Athens, Medea knew at once who he was. She managed to convince Aegeus that this newcomer had come to Athens to assassinate him. Theseus, worried by the cool way in which Aegeus received him, did not immediately let his father know who he was.

Medea persuaded Aegeus that the simplest way to dispose of this dangerous assassin was to poison him. She was a skilled hand with poisons.

"Invite this young man to the palace and drink a toast to him," she told Aegeus. "I will put aconite into the cup of wine from which he will drink in response."

All went as Medea had planned until, just as Theseus raised the cup of poisoned wine to his lips, Aegeus suddenly noticed the ivory hilt of Theseus's sword and recognized it as the one he had buried under the rock all those years ago. With a swift gesture he knocked the cup away from the lips of the son he saw for the first time and whom he now affectionately and gratefully embraced.

Aegeus gave a great feast for his son and newly proclaimed heir. Tales of the deeds performed by Theseus during his journey from Troezen to Athens were told over and over again. Theseus's deeds were compared with those performed by Herakles himself.

Medea had been afraid that Theseus might draw his sword with the ivory handle and kill her. So she hid herself in a magic cloud. But neither Theseus nor his father wanted revenge. Aegeus gave her an escort and urged her to leave the city. In any case it was no time to be bothering about Medea. There was a more threatening danger to think about.

It came from Pallas, the brother of Aegeus. As the years had gone by and Aegeus had failed to produce a son, Pallas, who had produced fifty giant sons, felt sure that he had only to wait for the throne of Athens to pass to his clan, the Pallantids. Now there had arrived this young upstart whom Aegeus had proclaimed to be his heir. The Pallantids decided to go to war.

Pallas himself, with twenty-five of his sons and many retainers, advanced against Athens, expecting that Aegeus and his men would march out to meet them. The other sons and their following waited in ambush. Fortunately Theseus was warned of the ambush by a herald of a clan that was supposed to be an ally of the Pallantids. Theseus was able to cut the ambush to pieces and Pallas retreated with his twenty-five remaining sons.

Theseus decided that his defeat of the Pallantids was not enough to impress Athens with his strength. He knew that there were many Athenians who still sympathized with Pallas, and he felt that it was imperative for him to prove himself a true Hero of Hellas. As it happened, a task was ready to hand.

One of the Labors of Herakles had been to capture a great white bull that was ravaging Crete, killing many of

Aegeus recognized Theseus as his lost son

the people. Eurystheus, the King of Tiryns, whom the Olympians had condemned Herakles to serve for 99 months, had ordered him to bring the savage bull from Crete to Tiryns. Herakles had succeeded in doing this, but Eurystheus stupidly let the bull loose again. It had ravaged the country around Argos, until finally the Argives had managed to drive it over the isthmus into Attica, where for some time now it had been killing many people and spoiling the crops on the plain of Marathon.

When Aegeus learned that his son and heir was set upon ridding the people of Marathon of this menace, he begged him not to attempt so rash a deed.

"Suppose it gores you to death. What will happen to me?"

"It will not gore me to death," Theseus replied confidently. "What Herakles once did I can do again. I overcame greater dangers on the way from Troezen, wearing your sandals and carrying your sword." And Aegeus realized that nothing he could say would change his son's mind.

On his way to Marathon, Theseus rested for a while in the hut of a poor old woman. Hecale, as she was called, was so old that Theseus seemed to her only a small boy. Theseus was not offended when she treated him like a child, but he thought that it would be as well if he told her what had brought him to Marathon.

"You are going to fight with that dreadful bull?" she gasped. "What can I do to stop you?"

"You will not stop me from trying my strength with the Marathonian bull," Theseus told her.

"All I have in the world is one ram, but if you come back safely I shall sacrifice it to Zeus to give thanks."

It is sad to know that when Theseus did come back safely the old woman was dead, but he was so grateful to her that he instituted annual rites in honor of Hecale and of Zeus; these were still being performed in Athens when the great battle of Marathon was fought many hundreds of years later.

We do not know the details of the struggle between Theseus and the savage white bull, only that Theseus succeeded in capturing the bull, bringing it to Athens, and dragging it up the steep path to the Acropolis, where he solemnly sacrificed it to Apollo.

Nevertheless, in spite of the feasting, a gloom was casting its shadow over Athens. The reason for this was that the time was fast approaching when a tribute of seven young men and seven young maidens would be demanded by the merciless King Minos of Crete.

Some years before, one of King Minos's sons, Androgeus, had competed in the Athenian Games, and had won contest after contest—boxing, wrestling, throwing the discus, and the rest. Then he had mysteriously disappeared. It was said that he had been murdered by some of his beaten rivals in the Games. But King Minos was not satisfied with this explanation and he finally discovered what had really happened. The truth was this.

The bull of Marathon

Androgeus had been so friendly with the Pallantids that King Aegeus had feared that he might persuade Minos to support a rebellion by Pallas and his fifty sons. Aegeus knew that he would inevitably lose the throne of Athens if King Minos brought his powerful fleet to help the Pallantids. So when he heard that Androgeus planned to go on to Thebes to take part in the games there, Aegeus thought of a plan. On his way to Thebes, Androgeus would have to pass through the city of Megara. Aegeus persuaded the Megareans to lay an ambush for Androgeus and take him prisoner. His idea was to prevent further intrigue with the Pallantids and to obtain from Androgeus a promise not to seek his father's support for a rebellion. However, Androgeus had fought desperately and had chosen to lose his life rather than surrender.

King Minos wasted no time in avenging his son's death. He first destroyed Megara, then he moved against Athens. At this time Crete was all-powerful in the small world of long ago and Aegeus realized that, unless he could come to terms with Minos, Athens would be destroyed as Megara had been.

The terms exacted by King Minos were grim indeed. Every ninth year—or according to some accounts, every year—seven youths and seven maidens were to be chosen by lot and sent to Crete. There they would be taken to the Labyrinth—the great maze built by Daedalus for King Minos under the palace at Knossos. In the heart of the Labyrinth lived the Minotaur, a monster with the body of a man and the head of a bull that fed on human flesh. The young Athenians thrown into the Labyrinth would have no hope of finding their way out and would either be eaten by the Minotaur or starve to death.

The sorrowful day came when the lots were to be drawn. Mothers were already weeping as they prayed to the gods of Olympus not to let any of their own sons or daughters be chosen. Theseus was so much moved by the townspeople's sorrow that he told his father he would volunteer to be one of the seven young men to go. Aegeus was horrified by the suggestion.

"But, my dear son, you will be going to certain death," he protested. "Not one young man or maiden sent to Crete as tribute has ever returned. All have been devoured by the Minotaur or have died of hunger because they could not find their way out of the Labyrinth."

"I mean to kill the Minotaur. If I could overcome the savage bull of Marathon I can surely overcome a bull with the body of a man or a man with the head of a bull. What is more, I shall persuade King Minos to remit the tribute if I succeed in slaying the Minotaur."

Aegeus continued to protest.

"It is useless to argue any more, father. I intend to go."

When the lots had been drawn, Theseus led his thirteen companions to the Dolphin Temple, where he offered to Apollo, on behalf of them all, a branch of olive tied with wool. The mothers of the thirteen had brought provisions for the voyage. Stifling their tears, they tried to make their

Victims for the Minotaur

sons and daughters feel less unhappy by telling them stories about the brave deeds of Hellenic Heroes.

The ship in which the young Athenians were to embark had black sails.

"Let us make some white sails also," Theseus said to his father. "When I come back in triumph after killing the Minotaur, our ship will carry white sails and you will know when you see them that the threat to Athens is for ever a thing of the past."

"You are more confident about the future than I am," Aegeus told his son. "Much more confident," he sighed. "But you shall have the white sails."

"The Delphic Oracle has told me to trust in the help of the goddess Aphrodite," Theseus said. "Before we go on board I shall sacrifice to her on the beach."

True to his promise, Theseus sacrificed a goat to Aphrodite, and prayed for her help in the task before him.

The ship with the black sails put to sea in April. This month was chosen because the weather was then more likely to be fine than in any other month except October. Boreas, the North Wind, can make himself very unpleasant over that sea in other months. The Athenians, who would one day become the most skilled navigators in Hellas, were at this time inferior sailors to the Cretans, who were then masters of the seas.

After a voyage of some days, the ship reached Knossos, the capital of Crete. King Minos rode down to the quay to make sure that the fourteen young men and women had safely arrived. He then ordered them to be locked up until the time came to send them into the Labyrinth.

It was when Theseus and his thirteen companions were being led away to prison that Aphrodite intervened as the Oracle had prophesied. Among those watching the sad procession to the prison were the young daughters of King Minos, Ariadne and Phaedra. Into the heart of the beautiful Ariadne, Eros, the boy god of love, shot one of his mischievous arrows. And Ariadne fell so wildly in love with Theseus that she determined to rescue him.

That evening she persuaded the guards of the prison to let her in, and to Theseus she said:

"If I help you to kill the Minotaur and escape with your companions from Knossos, will you promise to take me with you to Athens and marry me?"

Theseus was taken aback for a moment, but he quickly guessed that Aphrodite was helping him with the power of love, and at once he gave his promise.

Daedalus, the builder of the Labyrinth, had been very fond of the young daughters of King Minos. He had enjoyed making for them ingenious toys and mechanical dolls. When his longing to see once more his home in Athens made him decide to escape from Crete, he had given Ariadne a strange parting present. It was a ball of thread which, Daedalus explained, would show her how to find her way into the Labyrinth and out again. Ariadne felt that Daedalus must somehow have divined why she would need this ball of thread one day.

Theseus and his companions set sail for Crete

"I have the key of the door to the Labyrinth. I took it out of my father's belt while he slept. I will show you what to do when we come to the door."

The prison guards allowed Theseus to leave with Ariadne. They had a great affection for the beautiful young princess and, knowing the King was asleep, they were not afraid of being punished for letting Theseus leave with her. Ariadne led the way to the entrance to the Labyrinth. She explained to Theseus that he must tie the end of the ball of thread to the handle of the door and that the thread would then roll along until it reached the heart of the Labyrinth. Here, at midnight, the Minotaur would be sleeping. Every day, at this time, he slept for exactly an hour; he was never asleep at any other time. When he had killed the Minotaur Theseus would be able to find his way out of the Labyrinth by following the thread and rolling it into a ball again.

"I will be waiting for you to come out," Ariadne said. "And then we will all escape. But how will you kill the Minotaur?" she added anxiously. "In my haste I did not bring the sword I meant to give you."

"You are sure the Minotaur will be asleep at midnight?"

"Yes, but only for an hour."

"He will not wake up tomorrow morning," Theseus promised. "I have an unusually strong pair of wrists."

People who were inclined to be jealous of Theseus used to say he was boasting when he claimed to have throttled the Minotaur with his two hands. They declared that he must have had a sword. I think we can take Theseus's word that he did in fact throttle the Minotaur.

When Theseus came back with the ball of thread Ariadne threw her arms around his neck and kissed him, begging him to take her back to Athens with him. Theseus assured her that he would. He was naturally grateful to her for what she had done, but he was not as much in love with her as she was with him.

We do not know just how Theseus and Ariadne managed to persuade the guards to let Theseus's companions leave the prison and go down to the harbor. What we do know is that before they went on board their own ship with the black sails Theseus and the other young men bored holes in the Cretan ships at the quayside. They knew that if these ships pursued their little ship, it would undoubtedly be sunk. As it was, the Cretan ships did sail in pursuit, but they soon filled with water and sank.

In fine weather Theseus and his companions sailed northward until they came to the island of Naxos in the middle of the Cyclades, where Theseus decided to put in and go ashore for food and water. Then he made a strange decision. He suddenly ordered the ship to set sail from Naxos leaving Ariadne behind. Why? Perhaps the most plausible explanation of his action is that he had sighted a fleet of ships approaching and supposed that King Minos himself was at hand.

Ariadne had fallen asleep among the poppies in a field above the shore. She woke to find herself alone. You can

In the Labyrinth the Minotaur waited

imagine what she felt when she realized that Theseus had abandoned her on this unfamiliar island. She thought of what she had done for him by helping him to kill the Minotaur and save himself and his companions from the wrath of her father. What was to happen to her? Her father would never let her come back to Crete. She burst into a passion of tears and for an hour or more she bemoaned the cruel fate that had overtaken her. Suddenly, while she lay there sobbing, a handsome young man appeared and looked sympathetically down at her.

"Why are you weeping, Ariadne?" he asked.

She stared at him, wondering how he could have guessed her name. Then in an instant she became aware that this was no ordinary young man and that a kind of glowing influence seemed to surround him.

"Who are you?" she asked, feeling herself melting under that glowing influence.

"I am Dionysos, the god of wine."

As he spoke, there came across the fields a merry band of dancing satyrs, with old Silenus at their head, and a bevy of Maenads, all obviously excited by wine.

"Drink this, and you will not feel so sad," said Dionysos, offering Ariadne a goblet of wine. She no longer felt abandoned and alone.

'You are going to marry me," Dionysos told her, and at once all the satyrs with their goats' legs and hooves began to dance about more merrily than ever and the Maenads sang in a loud chorus. The marriage took place as soon as

Dionysos had placed upon the head of his bride a beautiful crown of rubies. Ariadne was happy again.

Meanwhile, Theseus had sailed from Naxos to the sacred isle of Delos. Here he sacrificed to Apollo and instituted games consecrated to the god. There was a palm tree growing on Delos, and Theseus started the custom of crowning the victor of the games with palm leaves.

It was on Delos that Theseus heard of the marriage of Dionysos and Ariadne, and he made up his mind that when he returned to Athens he would dedicate to them a festival at the time of the vintage. That annual festival was still being celebrated in Athens 2,000 years later.

When at last Theseus was ready to set off for Athens, the north wind blew fiercely day after day, and it was October before he sighted the shores of Attica. The ship was still carrying black sails; by some bitter mischance the white ones had not been hoisted.

Day after day King Aegeus had watched from a cliff-top for the appearance of his son's ship. He had prayed to all the gods that one happy day he would see it returning with white sails set. So when, on that October morning, he saw a ship with black sails approaching Athens, he was so overcome with disappointment and grief that he flung himself over the cliff. From that sad moment the sea into which he plunged to his death has been known as the Aegean Sea.

Theseus was not told of his father's death until he had sacrificed to the gods in gratitude for his safe return.

"I am Dionysos, the god of wine"

Theseus now succeeded to the throne of Athens. His one-time fellow-citizens of Troezen were so much impressed by his heroic deeds that they dedicated a sanctuary to him; the cost of the sacrifices was contributed by the parents of the thirteen young Athenians who had gone to Crete with Theseus and, but for him, would never have returned home alive.

Theseus proved to be a good king; upon the foundations of his wise rule the future greatness and glory of Athens were built. Until he came to the throne the various communities, or demes, of Attica had all been independent. Theseus managed to weld them together in what could be called the first commonwealth in history.

This was not the end of his adventures. He and his friend Peirithous went off to visit the land of the Amazons on the northeast shores of the Black Sea. The Amazons were a formidable tribe of women who could fight as well and as bravely as men. They received the two warriors with hospitality and friendliness and their Queen, Antiope, came on board Theseus's ship, bringing with her rich gifts. She must have had a great attraction for Theseus, because he carried her off in his ship, and when they reached Athens he married her.

The sister of Antiope, Oreithyia, was so angry at the abduction that she made an alliance with the Scythians and invaded Hellas with an army of Amazons and Scythians. The army reached Athens and there was a fierce battle on the outskirts of the city. The right wing of the Athenian army was overrun by the Amazons, but the left wing, commanded by Theseus, drove the enemy back.

Antiope rode and fought beside Theseus until she was killed by an arrow shot by one of the Amazons. Oreithyia was so overcome by the death of her sister, whom she had supposed to be in need of rescue from an enforced and unhappy marriage, that she rode away from the battlefield to die of grief in Megara. The rest of the Amazons gave up the struggle with Athens and went back with their allies to settle in Scythia.

Some years later Theseus married Phaedra, the younger sister of Ariadne. By her he had two sons, Demophoön and Akamas. He already had a son, Hippolytus, by Antiope. He was anxious that either Demophoön or Akamas should inherit the throne of Athens, and that Hippolytus should one day become King of Troezen, where he himself had been born and spent his youth. So he sent Hippolytus to Troezen, where he was warmly welcomed by King Pittheus, who at once adopted him as his heir.

Hippolytus had been taught by his mother to venerate the virgin goddess Athene, and he dedicated to her a temple in Troezen, near the gymnasium, where he spent much of his time training himself to become as great an athlete as his father.

The goddess Aphrodite was jealous of her Olympian sister Athene, who was inclined to be both critical and superior. When this handsome youth dedicated a temple

Queen Antiope brought rich gifts to Theseus

to Athene, Aphrodite resented it and decided to show her own power. So she made Phaedra fall in love with Hippolytus. Soon afterward, Hippolytus stayed in Athens after attending the Mysteries at Eleusis, at a time when Theseus was away. Phaedra wrote to Hippolytus begging him to go away with her while Theseus was absent. Hippolytus was horrified. He went to his stepmother's room to burn the letter and to reproach her. Phaedra, who was really mad with love, left a letter accusing Hippolytus of making love to her, and then hanged herself.

The news of this tragedy was brought to Theseus, who cursed his son and forbade him ever to come near him again. Hippolytus set off for Troezen in a four-horsed chariot but, as he was crossing the Isthmus, a monster appeared out of the sea. The horses panicked. Hippolytus lost control of his chariot, was flung out, became entangled in the reins, and was dragged along until he crashed into a rock by the roadside and was killed.

Only then did Theseus learn, from Athene, that Hippolytus was innocent of any offence. He was overcome with guilt and remorse at the thought that his curse had been responsible for the death of his son.

Perhaps Theseus's mind was affected by the dreadful fate of Phaedra and Hippolytus. At any rate, he fell in with a suggestion by his companion-in-arms, Peirithous, that they should go to Sparta and kidnap Helen, the daughter of Leda by Zeus and sister of the Heavenly Twins Kastor and Polydeukes. It is difficult otherwise to account for the folly of one who had hitherto ruled Athens so wisely and so well. The kidnapping of Helen was to start a fatal rivalry between Athens and Sparta that endured for hundreds of years.

Before they set out on their mad enterprise, the two friends agreed on oath that if they succeeded in kidnapping Helen they would draw lots to decide which of them should marry her when she was old enough. They also agreed that the winner would help the loser to wed another of the daughters of Zeus. They succeeded in stealing Helen from the temple of Artemis in Sparta and in evading pursuit by her brothers. Theseus was the winner when he and Peirithous drew lots. Knowing that the Athenians would resent his incurring the enmity of Kastor and Polydeukes, he hid Helen in a village in Attica, where his mother Aethra looked after her.

Helen remained successfully hidden away in that village until she was old enough to be married. She was now of the greatest beauty; indeed, she was soon to become the most beautiful woman in Hellas.

Theseus realized that he could not marry Helen without first appeasing her brothers. But while he was trying to think of a way of achieving this, Peirithous arrived in Athens and, no doubt a little jealous of his friend's prospect of marrying this beautiful daughter of Zeus, reminded Theseus of the agreement they had sworn.

"Remember that the winner was to help the loser to win another daughter of Zeus," said Peirithous.

The death of Hippolytus

"I have not forgotten," Theseus replied, "but which daughter have you set your heart upon?"

Peirithous said he thought that an oracle of Zeus should be consulted; it was Zeus by whom they had sworn their oath. The oracle told Peirithous to go down to Tartarus and demand the hand of Persephone from her husband Hades. Theseus was horrified at the thought of undertaking such an impious quest but, reminded again of his oath, he reluctantly agreed to go with Peirithous to the Underworld.

No doubt Hades had learned of the object of their visit from his brother Zeus. When they arrived, he pointed to a bench and invited them to sit down. They did so, supposing, with some relief, that they were being hospitably received. But when they tried to move they found they could not; they were stuck fast to the bench. And stuck fast they remained for four years, from time to time being whipped by the Furies and bitten by Cerberus.

At last came the merciful day when Herakles came to the Underworld to accomplish his last Labor. He was greeted affectionately by Persephone, who was his half-sister. Persephone still remembered how Theseus had killed the wrestler Kerkyon and how grateful her mother Demeter had been for this deed, which cleared the way to Eleusis for her pilgrims. So now Persephone pleaded with Hades to let Herakles set Theseus free. Hades grimly consented and Herakles, using all his tremendous strength, managed to pull Theseus from the bench. But, however hard he tugged, he could not pull Peirithous free. So Peirithous remained for ever in the Underworld.

Theseus returned to Athens. He found it bitterly torn by political rivalries. While he was away, Kastor and Polydeukes had invaded Attica with an army of Spartans and Arcadians. They had found Helen and sent her back to Sparta and, their mission completed, had returned home across the isthmus. But they had left behind as regent of Athens the grandson of a man who had been banished by King Aegeus. This was Menestheus, who had much influence over the populace and was the first man we hear of in mythology who preached democracy.

Theseus was exhausted by those four years of torment in the Underworld. He dedicated a temple to Herakles the Deliverer, but he found it increasingly difficult to exercise any authority or even to preserve his dignity. At last he decided to abandon Athens and sail to Crete, where King Minos no longer ruled. After Theseus had slain the Minotaur, Minos had sailed to Sicily with a great fleet to bring Daedalus, the builder of the Labyrinth, back to Knossos. But Daedalus was too clever to allow himself to be captured. He managed to kill Minos by pouring boiling water on the king as he lay in his bath. Minos was then made a judge of the Underworld by his father Zeus.

Theseus set sail for Crete, but a storm blew his ship from its course and he landed on Skyros, one of the islands of a small archipelago north of the Cyclades.

Treachery ended the life of Theseus

The ruler of Skyros, King Lykomedes, was a great friend of Menestheus, but he received Theseus cordially enough, and Theseus was soon captivated by the peaceful atmosphere of the island. He told Lykomedes that he might settle on the island, on a small estate that had been given to him. Lykomedes seemed to encourage the idea and suggested showing his guest the extent of his property. Under this pretext, Lykomedes enticed Theseus to the edge of a high cliff. There, treacherously, he pushed Theseus, who was grievously weakened by his years of torment in Tartarus, over the cliff to his death.

The Skyriots for a long time refused to reveal where on the island they had buried Theseus's body, and the people of Athens made no great attempts to find out. But at the battle of Marathon—when 10,000 Athenian soldiers, with a thousand brave volunteers from the little city of Plataea beside them, drove back the Persian hosts to win the greatest victory against odds in human history—the spirit of Theseus appeared to the Athenians, urging them to stand fast. After that, another effort was made to discover Theseus's burial place in Skyros. At last it was found, a stone coffin containing the skeleton of a tall man with a bronze spear and sword. The bones were taken back to Athens, where the Theseum was built as a sanctuary for them. The Theseum is still to be seen today. It has not the magnificence of the Parthenon, but it is a building that holds within it so much of the spirit of the earliest days of Athens that it still links us to that world of long ago.

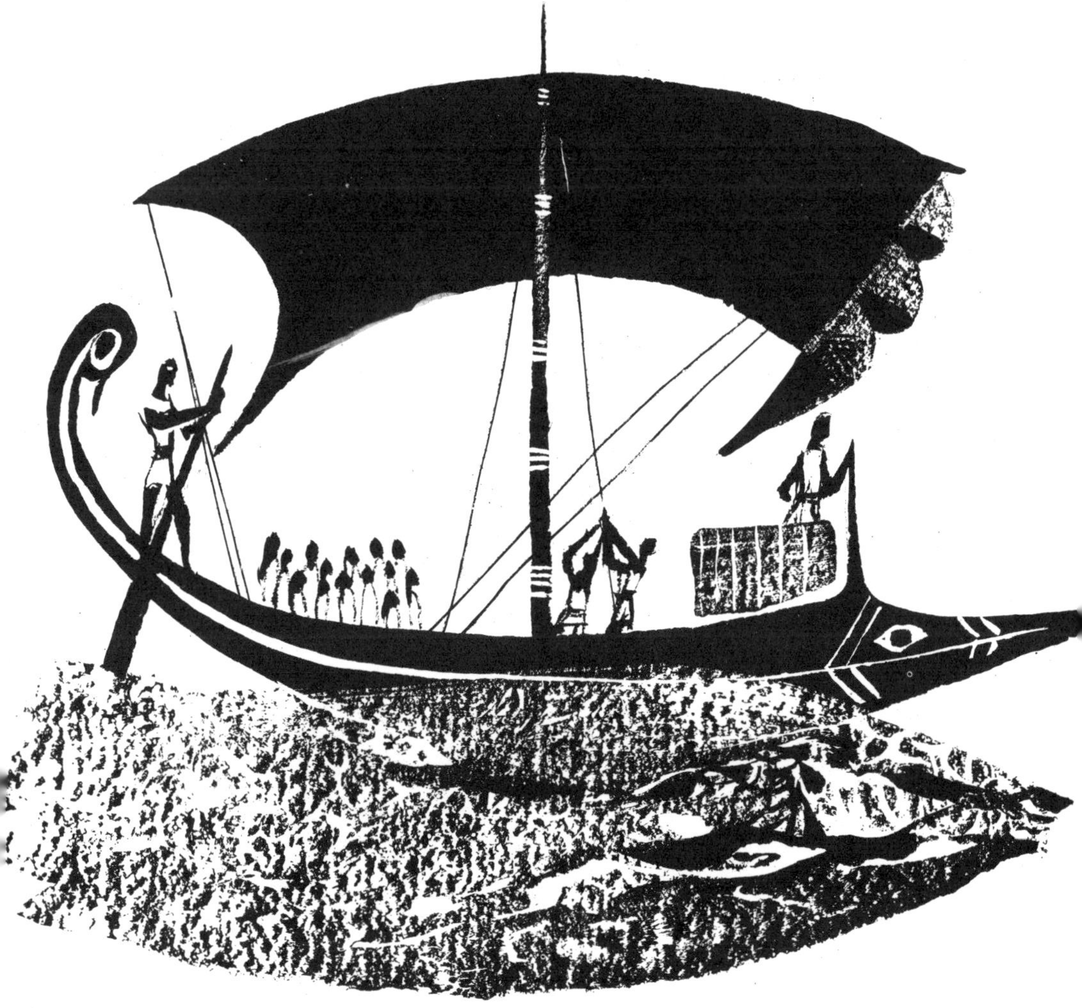

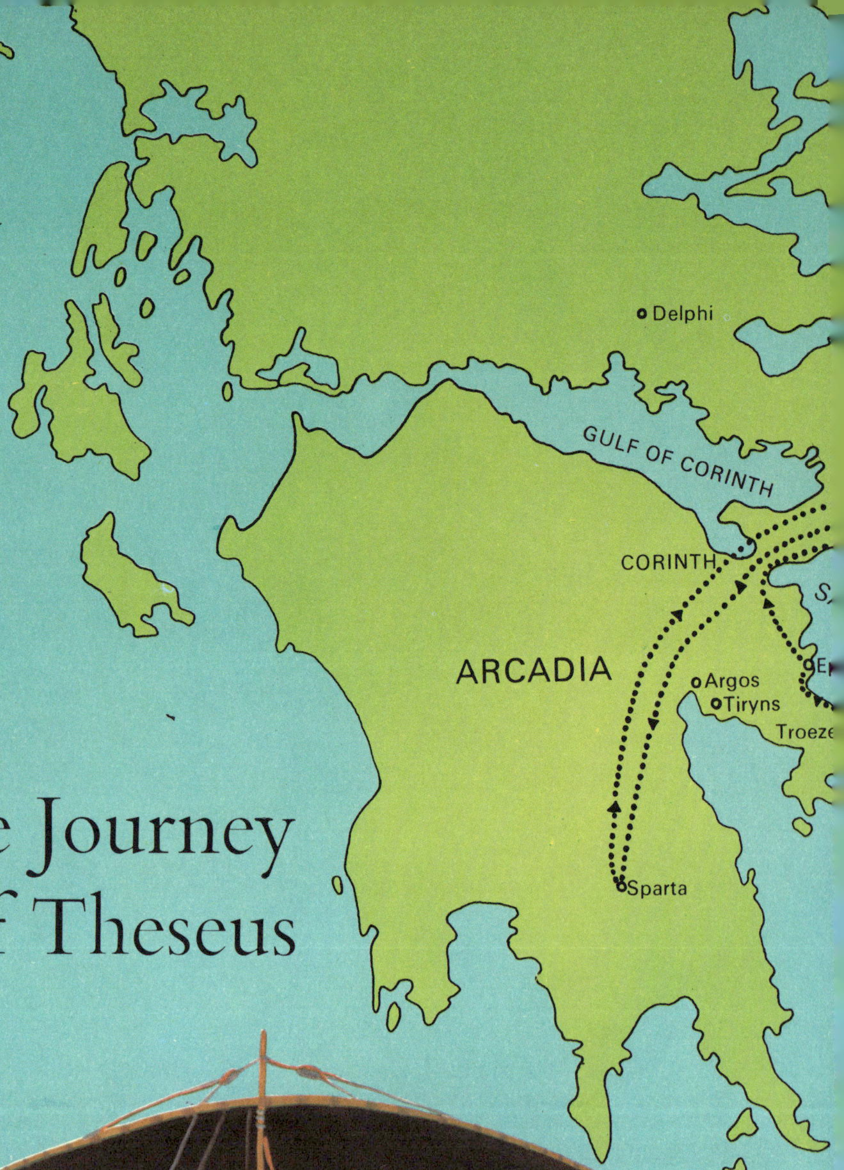

The Journey of Theseus

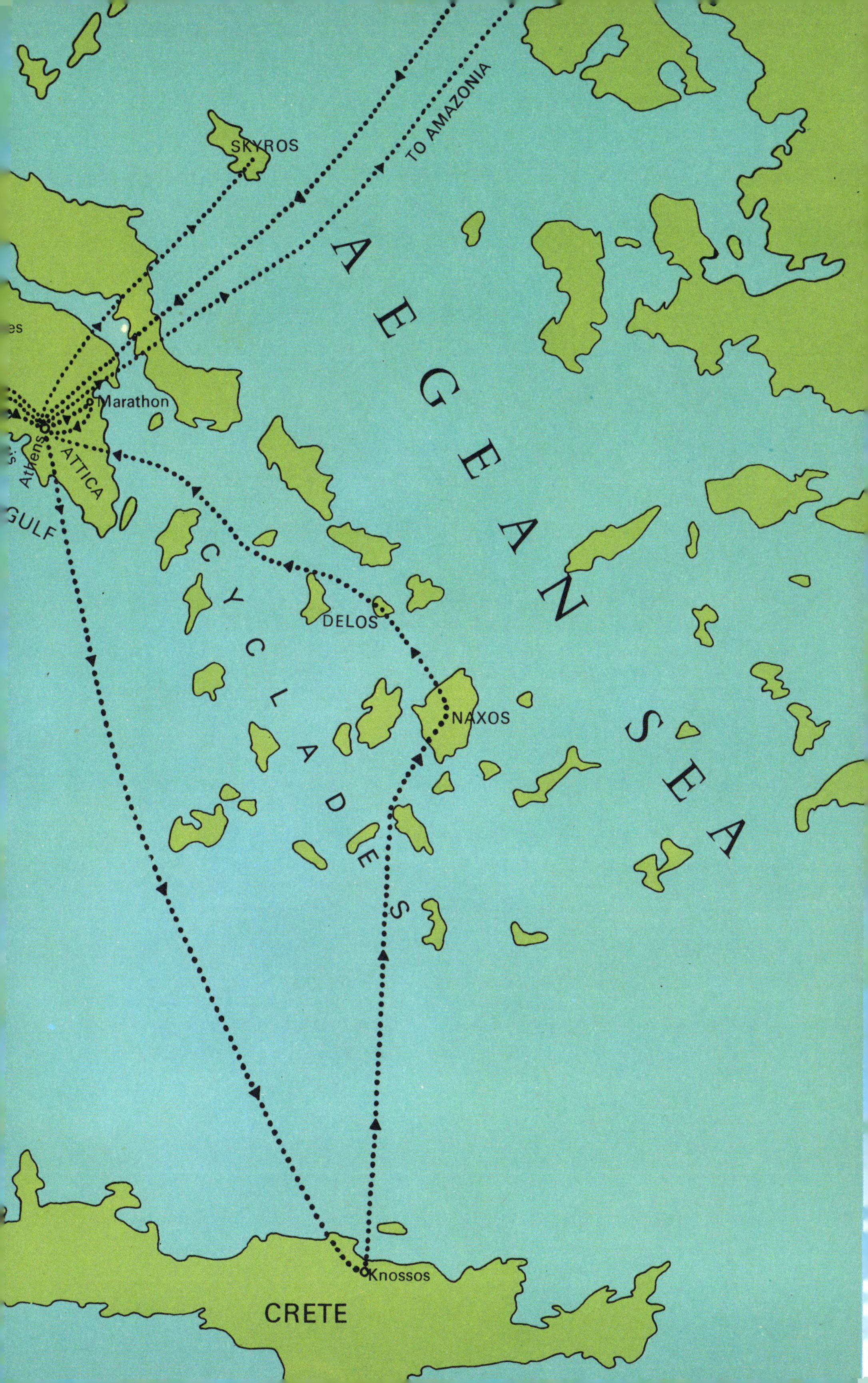

SKYROS
TO AMAZONIA
AEGEAN SEA
Marathon
Athens
ATTICA
GULF
CYCLADES
DELOS
NAXOS
Knossos
CRETE